Loving Someone with Complex PTSD

A Compassionate Guide to Understanding, Supporting, and Thriving in Your Relationship with a Childhood Trauma Survivor

Mable Jacquard McGowan

Table of Contents

Preface

The moment you realize your partner carries invisible wounds from childhood, everything shifts. Suddenly, patterns that seemed inexplicable begin to make sense. The push and pull, the disproportionate reactions, the walls that go up precisely when intimacy deepens. You're not dealing with a difficult personality or a lack of love. You're witnessing the aftereffects of trauma that rewired your partner's nervous system before they had words to describe what was happening to them.

I wrote this guide because partners of Complex PTSD survivors are often forgotten. The clinical literature focuses on the trauma survivor. Therapy addresses their symptoms. Support resources center their experience. Meanwhile, the person sharing their life, their bed, their daily struggles, receives little guidance on how to understand what they're witnessing or how to sustain themselves through the long process of healing.

You are not a therapist. You should not try to become one. But your role matters enormously. Research consistently demonstrates that secure relationships provide a foundation for trauma recovery. Your consistent presence, your willingness to learn, your capacity to stay regulated when your partner cannot, all of these contribute to healing in ways that professional treatment alone cannot replicate. Love is part of the medicine, even when it feels invisible or rejected.

At the same time, this work takes a toll. Partners of trauma survivors face real risks to their own mental and physical health. Secondary traumatic stress, compassion fatigue, and burnout are occupational hazards of loving someone whose nervous system is wired for danger. Any guide that ignores your wellbeing does you a disservice. Throughout these pages, you will find equal attention paid to understanding your partner and to protecting yourself. Both matter. Both are necessary for the relationship to survive.

What follows is a comprehensive framework for understanding Complex PTSD from the partner's perspective. You will learn what C-PTSD is and how it differs from the PTSD most people have heard of. You will understand emotional flashbacks, those sudden regressions into childhood emotional states that can make your partner seem like a different person. You will learn about the Four F survival responses, Fight, Flight, Freeze, and Fawn, and how each shapes relationship dynamics. You will gain insight into the inner critic, toxic shame, and attachment wounds that drive so much of your partner's behavior.

Beyond understanding, you will find practical tools. Communication strategies for when trauma is activated. Approaches to physical intimacy that honor your partner's nervous system. Trigger management plans for daily life and difficult occasions. Boundary-setting frameworks that protect you without abandoning your partner. Guidance on building your support network and maintaining your own mental health.

The later sections address the path forward: evidence-based treatments for C-PTSD, when and how to pursue couples therapy, what recovery actually looks like, and the difficult question of when love alone is not enough. The appendices provide quick reference cards, worksheets, and resources for ongoing support.

I have written in plain language, avoiding clinical jargon while remaining grounded in current research. Citations throughout allow you to explore the evidence base if you wish. The case examples are composites, fictional illustrations drawn from common patterns, included to help you recognize your own experience reflected in these pages.

A word of honesty before you begin: this is not easy reading, and what it describes is not easy living. Loving someone with Complex PTSD requires patience measured in years, not months. It requires tolerating discomfort, sitting with ambiguity, and accepting that progress is nonlinear. There will be setbacks. There will be moments when you question whether you can continue.

There will also be moments of profound connection. Watching someone you love reclaim pieces of themselves that trauma stole. Experiencing the deepening trust that comes from weathering storms together. Building a relationship more honest and resilient than many partnerships that never faced such challenges.

Both realities are true. The difficulty and the hope. The exhaustion and the meaning. My aim is to honor both while giving you the understanding and tools to navigate the path ahead.

Chapter 1.0 When Love Meets Trauma

The morning Theodora found the diagnosis in her husband's therapy notes, everything she thought she knew about their marriage shifted. She wasn't snooping. Marius had asked her to grab his insurance card from his bag, and the papers had spilled out. "Complex Post-Traumatic Stress Disorder" stared back at her from the clinical assessment. For three years, she had wondered why the man who loved her so fiercely sometimes looked at her like she was a stranger. Why he could be warm and present one moment, then gone behind his eyes the next. Why their arguments about small things spiraled into something much bigger. Now she had a name for it. But a name is just a starting point. What she needed was a map.

1.1 Why You Picked Up This Book

You're reading these words because someone you love carries invisible wounds. Maybe you've known about their trauma for years. Maybe you just learned about it recently. Maybe you're not entirely sure what's wrong, but you know something is, and you've been searching for answers.

Perhaps you've noticed patterns that don't make sense. Your partner withdraws when things are going well. They apologize constantly for things that aren't their fault. They seem to expect you to leave, even though you've given them no reason to think you would. They can't seem to take in your love, no matter how many times you offer it.

Or maybe the challenges are more visible. Arguments that blow up out of nowhere. Mood shifts that feel like whiplash. Times when your partner seems to become a different person entirely, someone younger, more frightened, more reactive than the adult you know them to be.

You've probably tried to help. You've reassured them, over and over. You've walked on eggshells. You've gotten frustrated, felt guilty for that frustration, then tried harder. You've wondered if you're the problem. You've wondered if they'll ever change. You've wondered if love is supposed to feel this exhausting.

Here's what I want you to know: your experience is valid. Loving someone with Complex PTSD is one of the most challenging things a person can do. It requires patience that stretches you, understanding that pushes you to grow, and a kind of steady presence that can leave you depleted if you don't also care for yourself.

This book was written to support you too. Not instead of your partner, but alongside them. Because the research is clear: when partners understand C-PTSD, relationships improve. When partners have tools, both people suffer less. When partners take care of themselves, they can sustain the long journey of healing together (Monson et al., 2012).

1.2 What This Book Offers

Let me be direct about what you'll find in these pages and what you won't.

This book will give you a thorough understanding of Complex PTSD. You'll learn what it is, how it differs from other conditions, and why it creates such specific challenges in intimate relationships. Knowledge is power here. When you understand why your partner reacts the way they do, you stop taking it personally. You stop blaming yourself. You stop blaming them. You start seeing the trauma for what it is: an unwanted third presence in your relationship that neither of you invited but both of you must address.

This book will give you practical strategies. You'll learn how to communicate when trauma is activated. You'll learn how to support without rescuing. You'll learn how to set boundaries that protect you while maintaining connection with your partner. You'll learn to

5

recognize emotional flashbacks and respond in ways that help rather than accidentally harm.

This book will validate your experience. Throughout these chapters, you'll hear from other partners who have walked this path. You'll recognize yourself in their stories. You'll feel less alone.

This book will also push you toward your own self-care. That's not optional. Partners of trauma survivors are at significant risk for secondary traumatic stress, compassion fatigue, and burnout (Bride & Figley, 2009). You cannot pour from an empty cup. Your wellbeing matters, not just for you, but for the relationship itself.

What this book will not do is turn you into your partner's therapist. You're not qualified for that role (no offense), and even if you were, it would be inappropriate. Therapists maintain boundaries specifically because healing requires a certain kind of professional distance. You're too close, too invested, too affected by your partner's pain to be objective. And that's fine. That's what being a partner means.

This book also won't promise you a timeline. Healing from C-PTSD takes years, not months. Some symptoms may never disappear entirely. What changes is their intensity, their frequency, and their power over your partner's life. Progress is real, but it's slow and nonlinear. Anyone who promises you a quick fix is selling something.

1.3 Supporting Versus Rescuing

One of the most important distinctions you'll learn in this book is the difference between supporting your partner and trying to rescue them.

Supporting looks like: listening without fixing, validating their feelings, maintaining your own stability when they're dysregulated, encouraging professional help, respecting their autonomy, and creating safety through consistency.

Rescuing looks like: trying to solve all their problems, protecting them from any discomfort, making decisions for them, excusing harmful behavior, sacrificing your own needs entirely, and treating them as fragile rather than capable.

The impulse to rescue comes from love. When someone you care about is suffering, you want to make it stop. But rescuing actually undermines your partner's healing. It reinforces the message that they can't handle things themselves. It creates dependence rather than growth. It exhausts you and ultimately breeds resentment.

Consider Berenice, whose partner Erasmus struggled with severe anxiety rooted in childhood neglect. For years, Berenice handled everything that might stress him. She screened his emails, fielded difficult phone calls, and made excuses to family members when he couldn't attend gatherings. She thought she was helping. What she was actually doing was confirming Erasmus's belief that he couldn't cope with normal life. When she finally, with the help of her own therapist, began stepping back, Erasmus was initially angry. Then he was scared. But slowly, he began to develop his own capacity to face challenges. The relationship shifted from caretaker and patient to two adults navigating life together.

Supporting means believing in your partner's capacity to heal while accepting that the healing is their work to do.

1.4 Your Role Matters Enormously

Here's the good news in all of this: you matter. A lot.

Research on trauma recovery consistently shows that secure relationships are one of the most powerful factors in healing. The brain that was wounded in relationships can also be healed in relationships (Siegel, 2012). Your presence, your consistency, your love creates conditions that allow recovery to happen.

This doesn't mean you heal your partner. They heal themselves, with professional support. But you provide something therapists can't:

daily evidence that relationships can be safe. Every time you respond to their fear with calm. Every time you stay present when they push you away. Every time you repair after a rupture. You are literally helping their nervous system learn a new way of being in the world.

A landmark study by Johnson and colleagues found that Emotionally Focused Therapy, which works with couples, not just individuals, produced significant reductions in trauma symptoms (Johnson, 2002). The relationship itself became the vehicle for healing. Your partnership has that same potential.

But, and this is important, you can't do it alone, and you can't do it perfectly. Your partner also needs professional treatment. Your support enhances therapy; it doesn't replace it. And you will make mistakes. You'll get triggered yourself. You'll say the wrong thing. You'll lose patience. That's human. What matters is the overall pattern: consistent enough safety, frequent enough repair, steady enough presence over time.

1.5 The Paradox of Receiving Love

One of the most painful experiences for partners of C-PTSD survivors is offering love and having it rejected or deflected.

You say "I love you," and they say "Why?" or "You shouldn't." You give them a compliment, and they argue with it. You try to do something nice, and they seem uncomfortable, suspicious, or even upset. You reach for them, and they pull away.

This isn't about you. But that doesn't make it hurt less.

People with C-PTSD often have a core belief, installed by their trauma, that they are unlovable, unworthy, or fundamentally defective (Walker, 2013). When you love them, you are directly contradicting this belief. And the brain, especially the traumatized brain, tends to reject information that doesn't match its existing model of the world.

Think of it like trying to give a gift to someone who is absolutely certain they don't deserve gifts. They can't take it in. It doesn't compute. Sometimes they'll assume there's a catch. Sometimes they'll feel so uncomfortable that they push it away. Sometimes they'll accept it on the surface but feel unworthy underneath.

This is why your reassurance doesn't seem to "stick." It's not that your words don't reach them. It's that their internal operating system keeps overwriting the new information with the old programming.

The solution isn't to reassure harder. It's to be patient. Consistent evidence over time gradually updates the brain's expectations. Your partner may never fully believe they deserve love, but they can learn to tolerate receiving it. They can learn to let it in, even when the inner voice says they shouldn't.

Faustina described this process beautifully: "My partner tells me I'm enough about a hundred times a week. For the first two years, I couldn't hear it at all. Now, maybe one in twenty times, something opens up and I actually feel it. That's progress. I hope someday it'll be one in ten, then one in five. We're working on it together."

1.6 How To Use This Book

This book is organized in six parts, designed to take you from understanding to action to sustainability.

Part One gives you the foundational knowledge about C-PTSD. You'll learn what it is, how it differs from regular PTSD, and why emotional flashbacks are the central challenge.

Part Two explores the Four F responses: Fight, Flight, Freeze, and Fawn. These are the survival adaptations your partner developed in childhood, and they directly affect your relationship. Understanding which patterns your partner tends toward will help you respond more effectively.

Part Three addresses the hidden enemies: the inner critic, toxic shame, and attachment wounds. These are the internal experiences that drive so much of C-PTSD's relationship difficulties.

Part Four offers practical strategies for daily life: communication, intimacy, parenting, and managing triggers.

Part Five is for you. It covers secondary traumatic stress, boundaries, building support, and protecting your own mental health.

Part Six looks at the path forward: treatment options, couples therapy, recovery possibilities, and knowing your limits.

You can read straight through, or you can jump to the sections most relevant to your current situation. Each chapter stands alone while also building on what came before. I'll reference earlier chapters when concepts connect, so you can track back if needed.

Throughout, you'll find practical tools, real stories (with names changed), and specific language you can use. This is meant to be useful, not just informative.

1.7 A Note on Pronouns and Relationships

C-PTSD affects people of all genders, orientations, and relationship structures. Throughout this book, I'll vary pronouns and try to include diverse examples. If a particular example doesn't match your situation, please adapt it to fit. The principles apply regardless of whether your partner is male, female, or nonbinary; whether you're married, dating, or somewhere in between; whether you're in a heterosexual or same-sex relationship.

What matters is the dynamic, not the demographics. You love someone who carries wounds from chronic early trauma. That's the common thread.

1.8 Moving Forward Together

10

As you begin this journey of understanding, hold onto three truths:

Your love matters, even when it seems rejected. Every act of consistent care is evidence that rewrites your partner's expectations about relationships. Even when they can't take it in, it's still doing something.

Understanding C-PTSD changes everything. Once you see the trauma for what it is, you stop fighting with symptoms and start addressing root causes. Knowledge transforms confusion into compassion.

You can't fix your partner, but you can create conditions for healing. Your role is to be a safe presence, not a savior. That's actually the more powerful position, because it respects your partner's agency and builds their capacity rather than fostering dependence.

The road ahead is long. There will be hard days and setbacks. But there will also be moments of profound connection, of seeing your partner grow stronger, of knowing that your commitment made a difference. Many couples navigate C-PTSD successfully. Their relationships become deeper, more honest, more resilient than many partnerships that never faced such challenges.

Theodora, from our opening story, would tell you that five years later, her marriage is better than it's ever been. Not easier, necessarily. But more real. Marius still has hard days. So does she. But they face them together now, with understanding, with tools, with hope.

That can be your story too.

1.9 Key Points

Your love matters, even when it seems rejected. Every act of consistent presence builds evidence that relationships can be safe.

Understanding C-PTSD changes everything. Knowledge transforms confusion into compassion and helps you stop taking symptoms personally.

You can't fix your partner, but you can create conditions for healing. Your role is to be supportive and steady, not to rescue or cure.

Chapter 2.0 Complex PTSD Explained

Gawain spent two years in therapy for depression before a new clinician finally asked about his childhood. He'd mentioned it in passing to previous therapists. The unpredictable father. The mother who was physically present but emotionally absent. The years of walking on eggshells, never knowing which version of dad would come through the door. "That's trauma," the new therapist said gently. Gawain was confused. He hadn't been beaten, not really. He hadn't been sexually abused. He thought trauma meant something visible, something dramatic. But as the therapist explained Complex PTSD, Gawain felt, for the first time, that someone understood the shape of his pain.

2.1 What Is Complex PTSD

Complex Post-Traumatic Stress Disorder is a condition that develops in response to prolonged, repeated trauma, particularly when that trauma occurs in childhood and involves caregivers or other people in positions of trust and power (Herman, 1992).

The World Health Organization formally recognized C-PTSD in the ICD-11, published in 2018 and implemented in 2022. According to this diagnostic framework, C-PTSD includes all the symptoms of traditional PTSD, such as re-experiencing the trauma through flashbacks or nightmares, avoidance of trauma-related triggers, and heightened threat perception. But it adds three additional symptom clusters that reflect the deeper damage of chronic relational trauma (World Health Organization, 2019).

The first additional cluster is difficulty with emotional regulation. People with C-PTSD often experience intense emotions that feel overwhelming and hard to manage. They may swing from numbness to rage to despair with little warning. Their emotional responses often seem disproportionate to the situation at hand, because they're actually responding to something from the past, not the present.

The second cluster involves negative self-concept. This goes beyond low self-esteem. People with C-PTSD often have a deep, pervasive sense of being permanently damaged, worthless, or fundamentally different from other people. They may feel chronic shame, emptiness, or a sense of being contaminated by what happened to them.

The third cluster relates to relationship difficulties. People with C-PTSD often struggle with trust and intimacy. They may have difficulty feeling close to others or may become attached very quickly and intensely. They often expect betrayal or abandonment. They may avoid relationships entirely or stay in unhealthy ones because they believe they don't deserve better.

These three clusters, emotional dysregulation, negative self-concept, and relationship disturbances, capture what makes C-PTSD distinctly relational in nature. The trauma happened in the context of relationships, usually with caregivers during development. The damage, therefore, goes to the core of how a person experiences themselves and connects with others.

2.2 Why C-PTSD Is Not In The DSM

If you're in the United States, you may have noticed that your partner's diagnosis doesn't include the word "Complex." That's because the American Psychiatric Association's Diagnostic and Statistical Manual (DSM-5) does not recognize C-PTSD as a separate diagnosis.

This matters for practical reasons. Insurance companies use DSM codes. Many clinicians in the U.S. were trained primarily on the DSM. If your partner has been diagnosed with PTSD, depression, anxiety, or even borderline personality disorder, they may actually have C-PTSD that's being labeled as something else.

The DSM-5 task force considered adding C-PTSD but ultimately decided the evidence wasn't sufficient to establish it as distinct from PTSD (Friedman, 2013). Many trauma experts disagree with this decision. Research has consistently shown that people with histories of chronic interpersonal trauma present differently than those with single-incident trauma, and they often respond differently to treatment (Cloitre et al., 2013).

For your purposes as a partner, the distinction matters because treatment approaches differ. Standard PTSD treatments like Prolonged Exposure or Cognitive Processing Therapy focus heavily on processing specific traumatic memories. For C-PTSD, where the trauma was ongoing and relational, treatment often needs to prioritize building safety, developing emotion regulation skills, and addressing attachment wounds before memory processing can be effective (Cloitre et al., 2010).

If your partner has tried therapy "that didn't work," this may be why. They may have received treatment designed for single-incident trauma when they needed something more comprehensive and relational.

2.3 Emotional Dysregulation Up Close

The emotional life of someone with C-PTSD often feels like a roller coaster with no brakes.

Your partner may go from calm to furious in seconds. They may sob over something that seems minor. They may swing between needing you desperately and pushing you away completely. They may feel emotions so intensely that they become overwhelmed and shut down entirely.

This isn't weakness or manipulation. It's the legacy of a developing brain that was forced to adapt to unpredictable, threatening conditions (van der Kolk, 2014).

In healthy development, children learn to regulate their emotions through interaction with attuned caregivers. The caregiver notices the child's distress, responds with comfort, and the child's nervous system settles. Over thousands of these interactions, the child internalizes the capacity to soothe themselves. They develop what researchers call "affect tolerance," the ability to experience strong emotions without being overwhelmed by them.

When caregivers are themselves the source of distress, or when they're unavailable or inconsistent, this learning doesn't happen. The child's nervous system never fully develops the capacity for self-regulation. They grow into adults who can be flooded by emotion, who struggle to return to baseline after distress, who may either feel everything too intensely or shut down all feeling entirely.

Ianthe described her experience this way: "It's like everyone else has an emotional thermostat, and mine is broken. I'm either freezing or on fire. When I get upset, I can't find the dial to turn it down. I just have to wait until it burns out."

2.4 The Wound Of Negative Self Concept

Perhaps the cruelest aspect of C-PTSD is how it convinces survivors that they are the problem.

When bad things happen to us as adults, we generally understand, eventually, that we were victims of circumstance, malice, or bad luck. When bad things happen to us as children, at the hands of the people who are supposed to love and protect us, we reach a different conclusion. Children are developmentally incapable of seeing their caregivers as wrong. It's too threatening. So they conclude that they must be wrong instead. They must have deserved it. There must be something fundamentally bad about them (Herman, 1992).

This toxic shame, which we'll explore more deeply in Chapter 11, becomes the lens through which your partner sees everything. They interpret neutral events as confirmation of their badness. They discount evidence of their worth. They expect rejection because they believe they deserve it.

Your partner may say things like: "I don't know why you're with me." "You'd be better off with someone else." "I'm too broken to love." "There's something wrong with me that can't be fixed."

These aren't fishing for compliments. They're honest reports of internal experience. Your partner really believes these things. The belief was installed in childhood, reinforced by years of mistreatment, and calcified into what feels like absolute truth.

This is why reassurance alone doesn't help. You can't argue someone out of a core belief that was formed before they had words to articulate it. Change requires slow, patient work in therapy, combined with consistent contrary evidence in the form of your ongoing, imperfect, but steady love.

2.5 Relationship Disturbances

C-PTSD is, at its heart, a disorder of attachment.

The same caregivers who should have provided safety and nurturing were the source of harm. This creates what attachment researchers call a "disorganized" pattern: the child needs to approach the caregiver for comfort but also needs to flee from them for safety. There's no solution to this impossible equation. The child's system freezes, confused, unable to organize a coherent strategy for getting needs met (Main & Hesse, 1990).

Fast forward to adulthood, and this same pattern plays out in romantic relationships. Your partner desperately wants closeness but fears it. They may cling one moment and push away the next. They may test you to see if you'll leave, then feel unbearable when you don't because they don't know how to tolerate being loved. They may pick fights when things are going well, unconsciously creating the rejection they expect.

Osric's partner, Clotilde, described it as "loving someone who has one foot out the door, even when they swear they want to stay." For the first year of their relationship, Clotilde regularly threatened to

17

end things, seemingly out of nowhere. Eventually, through therapy, she recognized the pattern: whenever she started feeling close to Osric, panic set in. Closeness meant vulnerability. Vulnerability meant getting hurt. Pushing him away felt safer than waiting to be abandoned.

Understanding this pattern doesn't make it easy to live with. But it helps you see it for what it is: trauma logic, not relationship logic. Your partner isn't choosing to push and pull. Their nervous system is running a survival program written in childhood.

2.6 How Trauma Rewires The Brain

The developing brain is remarkably plastic, meaning it shapes itself according to its environment. This is wonderful when the environment is safe and nurturing. It becomes problematic when the environment is threatening.

Children who grow up with chronic stress show measurable changes in brain structure and function. The amygdala, the brain's alarm system, becomes hyperactive, constantly scanning for danger (Teicher & Samson, 2016). The prefrontal cortex, responsible for reasoning and impulse control, develops less fully, because survival required reaction speed, not careful thought. The hippocampus, which processes memory, may be smaller, contributing to fragmented or missing memories of the traumatic period (van der Kolk, 2014).

These changes served a purpose. A child living in an unsafe home needs to be hypervigilant. They need to react quickly when threat appears. They can't afford to stop and think; they need to act. The brain optimized for survival.

The problem is that these adaptations persist even when the danger is gone. Your partner's adult brain is still running the programming installed in childhood. It perceives threats that aren't there. It reacts before thinking. It struggles to distinguish past from present.

This is neurological, not psychological weakness. Your partner isn't choosing to be reactive any more than someone with a broken leg is choosing to limp.

The encouraging news is that brains remain plastic throughout life. With proper treatment, safety, and time, new neural pathways can develop. The alarm system can be recalibrated. This is slow work, measured in years, but it's real. Recovery is not just possible; it's documented in research (Cloitre et al., 2010).

2.7 Big T and Little T Trauma

People often think of trauma as dramatic events: war, assault, natural disasters. These are what clinicians sometimes call "Big T" traumas. They're visible, recognized, often sudden.

But trauma can also be quieter. "Little t" traumas are experiences that may not seem catastrophic from the outside but were deeply wounding to the person who experienced them. Chronic criticism. Emotional neglect. Unpredictability. Having a parent who was physically present but emotionally unavailable. Being the forgotten child in a chaotic family.

C-PTSD is often the result of accumulated "little t" traumas rather than a single devastating event. The damage comes from the drip, drip, drip of daily wounding over years of development. Each individual incident might not seem like much. Added together, they fundamentally alter a child's sense of self and safety (van der Kolk, 2014).

This is why your partner may struggle to point to "what happened." They may not have specific memories of abuse. They may wonder if they're making it up or being dramatic. They may say things like, "It wasn't that bad" or "Other people had it worse."

The body keeps score, as Bessel van der Kolk's influential book title suggests. Even without clear memories, the impacts are real: the hypervigilance, the shame, the relationship difficulties, the emotional flooding. These symptoms are evidence that something happened, even if the mind can't access the specifics.

2.8 When Childhood Seemed Normal

One of the most confusing aspects of C-PTSD for both survivors and their partners is when the traumatic childhood didn't look obviously bad.

Your partner may have grown up in a nice house in a good neighborhood. Their parents may have stayed married, attended school events, provided material needs. There may be no stories of dramatic abuse. Other people, even your partner themselves, may wonder what they have to complain about.

But trauma isn't always about what happened. Sometimes it's about what didn't happen. Emotional neglect, the absence of attunement, warmth, and connection, can be as damaging as active abuse (Webb, 2012). The child who is fed and clothed but never truly seen, whose emotions are dismissed or ignored, whose inner world is treated as unimportant, can develop C-PTSD just as surely as the child who was hit.

Dorothea's partner, Simeon, came from what everyone called "a good family." Successful parents, private school, family vacations. But his mother was cold and critical, his father emotionally absent, and Simeon learned early that his feelings were inconvenient and his needs were too much. In adulthood, he struggled to identify what he was feeling, couldn't ask for help without shame, and expected everyone to eventually find him disappointing. The neglect was invisible, but its effects were profound.

If your partner's childhood "didn't seem that bad," that doesn't mean their pain isn't real. Emotional neglect is particularly insidious because it leaves no visible marks. The absence of something needed for healthy development is just as impactful as the presence of something harmful.

2.9 Why Siblings Differ

It's common for partners to feel confused when their loved one has siblings who seem fine. If the family was so problematic, why isn't everyone affected?

The answer is that children in the same family don't actually have the same experience. Birth order matters; the oldest child may bear more responsibility or criticism, while the youngest may be overlooked. Different children may be assigned different roles: the golden child, the scapegoat, the invisible one. Temperament matters; some children are more sensitive and thus more deeply affected by the same treatment. Some children may have access to protective factors, like a grandparent, teacher, or friend, that buffer them from harm (Werner, 1995).

Your partner may have been particularly targeted by an abusive parent while a sibling was spared. Your partner may have had a temperament that made them more vulnerable to neglect. Your partner may have lacked the external supports that helped a sibling survive.

It's also possible that siblings were affected but show it differently. One person develops C-PTSD with obvious symptoms. Another develops workaholism and perfectionism (a flight response, as we'll discuss later). Another becomes the family peacekeeper, fawning to keep everyone happy. Another shuts down entirely and seems fine on the surface because they've dissociated from all emotion.

The fact that your partner's siblings seem okay doesn't invalidate your partner's experience. Each person's response to family dynamics is unique.

2.10 What Your Partner Carries

Understanding C-PTSD is understanding what your partner carries every day.

They carry a nervous system that is tuned for danger, constantly scanning for threats you can't perceive.

They carry an inner voice that criticizes them relentlessly, saying the things their caregivers said or implied until those messages became self-talk.

They carry a deep belief, beneath conscious awareness, that they are fundamentally broken, unworthy, and unlovable.

They carry the exhausting effort of trying to appear normal while managing internal chaos.

They carry the loneliness of feeling profoundly different from people who had "normal" childhoods.

And yet, your partner is also carrying something else: the determination to keep going, to seek healing, to try to love and be loved despite everything. That takes enormous courage. Many people with their history wouldn't have made it this far. Your partner did. They're here, trying to build a life with you.

That's what this book is for: helping both of you build that life together, with understanding, with tools, with hope.

2.11 Pulling It Together

C-PTSD is a normal response to abnormal circumstances. Your partner's brain and body adapted to survive chronic threat. Those adaptations, while problematic now, kept them alive then.

The brain adapted to survive, and now it needs to learn that it's safe. With proper treatment, consistent safety, and time, the nervous system can recalibrate. Recovery is real and documented.

Your partner isn't choosing these responses. The hypervigilance, the emotional flooding, the push-pull in relationships, these aren't personality flaws or manipulation. They're trauma symptoms. Understanding this changes how you respond to difficult moments.

Chapter 3.0 C-PTSD Versus Regular PTSD

When Julius returned from his second deployment, his wife Melisande knew what to expect. She'd read the books, attended the support group for military spouses, and prepared for the flashbacks and nightmares. She understood that fireworks would be hard and crowds might be triggering. What she didn't expect was how different her experience was from the other spouses in her group. Their partners seemed to improve with standard PTSD treatment. Julius got worse. It took another year and a new therapist to discover that Julius's real trauma wasn't combat. It was the childhood he'd never talked about, the one that had driven him to enlist in the first place. He didn't have PTSD. He had C-PTSD. And that changed everything.

3.1 The Core Difference

PTSD and C-PTSD share many features, but they are fundamentally different conditions that require different understanding and often different treatment.

Traditional PTSD typically develops after a single traumatic event or a discrete period of trauma. A car accident. An assault. A natural disaster. Combat deployment. The person's life had a "before" and "after" with a clear line between them. They can usually identify what happened and when (American Psychiatric Association, 2013).

C-PTSD develops from prolonged, repeated trauma, usually starting in childhood and typically involving abuse, neglect, or maltreatment by caregivers. There's no clear "before," because the trauma is interwoven with the person's development. The trauma isn't something that happened to an already-formed self. It shaped the self as it was forming (Herman, 1992).

This distinction matters enormously for your relationship because it affects what your partner struggles with and why.

3.2 Fear of Triggers Versus Fear of Relationships

A person with traditional PTSD fears specific triggers connected to their trauma. The combat veteran may fear loud noises, certain smells, or locations that remind them of war. The assault survivor may fear being alone, certain physical sensations, or situations similar to the attack. These triggers are identifiable, even if they're sometimes surprising in what sets them off.

A person with C-PTSD fears something far more fundamental: relationships themselves.

When trauma happens in the context of close relationships with caregivers, the message becomes: people who love you will hurt you. Intimacy is dangerous. Trust leads to betrayal. Need leads to rejection.

Your partner isn't afraid of you in the way a combat veteran is afraid of fireworks. They're afraid of what you represent: closeness, vulnerability, dependence. They're afraid of what relationships have always meant to them: pain, disappointment, abandonment.

This fear may not look like fear. It may look like picking fights. It may look like emotional distance. It may look like testing you. It may look like pushing you away when things are going well. But underneath, it's terror of the very thing they want most.

Leocadia realized this about her partner Quirin after years of confusion: "I kept thinking he was afraid of something specific, like I was going to do something to hurt him. But it wasn't about me at all. He was afraid of loving someone, period. He was afraid of needing anyone, because every time he'd needed someone before, they'd let him down."

3.3 Visual Flashbacks Versus Emotional Flashbacks

When most people hear "flashback," they imagine what's depicted in movies: the person is suddenly transported back to a specific traumatic scene. They see, hear, and smell what they experienced. They may not know where they are or confuse present circumstances for past events.

People with C-PTSD do sometimes experience these visual flashbacks, but more commonly they experience what Pete Walker calls "emotional flashbacks" (Walker, 2013). These are sudden regressions into the overwhelming emotional states of childhood trauma without any visual or cognitive component.

During an emotional flashback, your partner may suddenly feel small, helpless, terrified, or filled with shame. They may feel worthless, abandoned, or in danger. These feelings are intense and often seem to come from nowhere. There's no scene they're flashing back to, no clear connection to the past. They just suddenly feel awful in ways they can't explain or control.

This is confusing for partners because there's nothing visible to point to. Your partner can't say, "I'm remembering the time when..." because they're not remembering anything specific. They're experiencing a flood of emotion that's actually a body memory from the past, but it doesn't come with a narrative they can identify or share.

From the outside, emotional flashbacks look like sudden mood changes, overreactions, shutdowns, or inexplicable distress. You may find yourself asking, "What happened? What's wrong?" and your partner may not be able to tell you because they genuinely don't know. They just feel overwhelmed by feelings that seem to belong to someone else, someone younger and more helpless, which is exactly who they become during the flashback.

3.4 What Happened Versus Who I Am

Perhaps the most significant difference is in what the trauma affects.

With traditional PTSD, the trauma is something that happened to the person. They had an identity before the trauma and can conceptualize themselves as someone who experienced something terrible. The trauma is an event in their history, however painful.

With C-PTSD, the trauma shaped the person's identity. There's no sense of who they were "before" because the trauma was happening while they were becoming who they are. The damage isn't just to their sense of safety; it's to their sense of self.

This is why people with C-PTSD so often believe they're fundamentally defective rather than wounded. They don't think, "Something bad happened to me." They think, "I am bad." The shame isn't about what they experienced; it's about who they believe they are (Herman, 1992).

For partners, this means that healing isn't just about processing traumatic memories. It's about reconstructing your partner's entire sense of self, their beliefs about their worth, their capacity for healthy relationships, their right to exist and take up space in the world. This is longer, deeper work.

3.5 Trust Damaged Versus Trust Undeveloped

When someone experiences PTSD from an adult trauma, their basic trust in the world may be damaged. They had the experience of safety and then lost it. Recovery involves rebuilding what was broken.

When someone develops C-PTSD from childhood trauma, especially involving caregivers, basic trust may never have developed in the first place. There's nothing to rebuild because there was no foundation.

Attachment researchers describe this as insecure attachment, specifically the disorganized attachment style that is strongly associated with childhood abuse and neglect (Main & Hesse, 1990). The child needed their caregiver for survival but also needed to protect themselves from the caregiver. This impossible situation creates an internal chaos around attachment that persists into adulthood.

Your partner may never have experienced what it's like to trust someone completely. They may not know what secure attachment feels like. They may intellectually want to trust you but have no template for how that works.

This doesn't mean trust is impossible. But it does mean that your partner isn't "getting back to" a state of trust they once had. They're building it from scratch, as an adult, which is harder but absolutely achievable.

3.6 Common Misdiagnoses

C-PTSD is frequently misdiagnosed, partly because it isn't in the DSM-5 and partly because its symptoms overlap with other conditions. Understanding these misdiagnoses may help you make sense of your partner's treatment history.

Borderline Personality Disorder (BPD) shares many features with C-PTSD: emotional dysregulation, relationship difficulties, identity disturbance, fear of abandonment. Research shows that most people diagnosed with BPD have trauma histories, and some researchers argue that BPD is actually a form of C-PTSD (Ford & Courtois, 2014). The treatment implications differ: BPD treatment focuses heavily on skills training, while C-PTSD treatment must also address the trauma directly.

Bipolar Disorder may be diagnosed when clinicians observe the mood instability of C-PTSD without recognizing its trauma-driven nature. The rapid shifts from activation to shutdown can look like cycling between mania and depression. The distinguishing feature is that C-PTSD mood shifts are usually triggered by relational or environmental factors rather than occurring in predictable cycles.

Major Depression may be diagnosed when the symptoms of collapse, despair, and negative self-view are prominent. Many people with C-PTSD do experience depression, but treating only the depression doesn't address the underlying trauma.

Generalized Anxiety Disorder may be diagnosed when the hypervigilance and worry of C-PTSD are the most visible symptoms. Again, addressing anxiety without addressing trauma provides only partial help.

Some people are simply labeled as "difficult" or told they have a "personality disorder" without specific diagnosis. This can be harmful and shaming, adding to the trauma rather than addressing it.

If your partner has tried treatments for one of these conditions without success, C-PTSD may be the missing piece.

3.7 Treatment Differences

The good news about understanding C-PTSD as distinct from PTSD is that it points toward more appropriate treatment.

Standard PTSD treatments like Prolonged Exposure (PE) and Cognitive Processing Therapy (CPT) focus on processing specific traumatic memories. The person tells their trauma story repeatedly until it loses its emotional charge. These treatments are effective for many people with PTSD (Watkins et al., 2018).

For C-PTSD, jumping straight into trauma processing can actually be harmful. When trauma is developmental and relational, the person first needs to build capacity for emotional regulation and develop a safe therapeutic relationship. Only then can they tolerate examining traumatic material without being retraumatized (Cloitre et al., 2010).

The phase-based approach recommended for C-PTSD includes three stages: Safety and stabilization, building emotion regulation skills, creating safety in the therapy relationship, addressing current life problems. Trauma processing, carefully working through traumatic memories with the support developed in phase one. Integration and reconnection, consolidating gains, improving relationships, and building a life worth living.

Many trauma experts recommend treatments that address attachment and relationship patterns, such as EMDR (Eye Movement Desensitization and Reprocessing), Internal Family Systems (IFS), Schema Therapy, or attachment-focused approaches (Cloitre et al., 2011).

3.8 Why Old Therapy Did Not Work

If your partner has tried therapy before without much progress, this may explain why.

They may have received treatment for the wrong diagnosis. Depression or anxiety treatment doesn't address underlying trauma. Even PTSD treatment that focuses on specific memory processing may not help with developmental trauma.

They may have experienced a therapist who moved too fast. A well-meaning clinician who pushes trauma processing before the client has stabilized can cause retraumatization rather than healing.

They may have had a therapist who didn't understand relational trauma. The therapy relationship is crucial for C-PTSD recovery. A therapist who is clinical and distant, however competent, may not provide the corrective relational experience that's needed.

They may have encountered therapists who minimized their experience. "That doesn't sound that bad" or "Everyone had a difficult childhood" can reinforce the survivor's own tendency to dismiss their pain.

The right therapist and the right approach make an enormous difference. Your partner's past therapy failures are not evidence that they can't be helped. They're evidence that they hadn't yet found the right help.

3.9 Comparison At A Glance

Traditional PTSD typically involves a single event or discrete trauma period. C-PTSD involves prolonged, repeated trauma, usually in childhood.

Traditional PTSD fear centers on specific triggers related to the traumatic event. C-PTSD fear centers on relationships and intimacy themselves.

Traditional PTSD flashbacks are usually visual and sensory, with clear connection to the event. C-PTSD flashbacks are often emotional, without visual content, and disconnected from specific memory.

Traditional PTSD affects sense of safety in the world. C-PTSD affects the core sense of self.

Traditional PTSD damages previously developed trust. C-PTSD prevents trust from developing in the first place.

Traditional PTSD treatment focuses on processing the traumatic memory. C-PTSD treatment requires phased approach with stabilization before processing.

3.10 What This Means For You

Understanding that your partner has C-PTSD, not just regular PTSD, changes how you approach the relationship.

You stop waiting for them to identify "what happened." The trauma wasn't an event. It was an environment. There may be no single story to tell.

You adjust your expectations for recovery timeline. C-PTSD healing is measured in years, not months. The damage is deeper, and repair takes longer.

You recognize that the relationship itself is the arena of both wounding and healing. Your partner's fears about intimacy aren't irrational; they're based on their entire developmental experience. Your consistent safety gradually teaches them something new.

You support finding the right treatment. Standard approaches may not help. Phase-based, attachment-focused, trauma-informed treatment is what the research supports.

You understand that some of what you're dealing with isn't about you at all. Your partner's push-pull, their difficulty receiving love, their defensive reactions are responses to developmental trauma playing out in the present.

3.11 What We Covered

The trauma happened in relationships, so healing often triggers relationship fears. Your partner isn't afraid of something specific; they're afraid of the closeness you offer, because closeness has always meant pain.

C-PTSD affects identity, not just memory. Your partner doesn't believe something bad happened to them. They believe they are bad. This requires deeper, longer healing than processing a traumatic event.

Treatment needs to address attachment, not just symptoms. The right therapy, with the right approach and the right therapist, can make all the difference.

Chapter 4.0 Emotional Flashbacks Explained

The dishes had been sitting in the sink for two days. Honora mentioned it to her husband Remigius, not critically, just noting that they needed to be done. His reaction stunned her. He went pale, then flushed red. His voice changed, becoming younger and more desperate. "I know, I know, I'm sorry, I'll do them right now, please don't, I'm sorry." He was shaking. Over dishes. Honora stood frozen, not knowing what had just happened. Later, after he'd calmed, Remigius couldn't explain it either. "I don't know what came over me. I just suddenly felt like I was going to be hit." He hadn't been hit since he was twelve years old. But in that moment, he was twelve again, and Honora was his raging father, and the dirty dishes were evidence of his failure as a human being.

4.1 What Emotional Flashbacks Are

Emotional flashbacks are the signature symptom of Complex PTSD, and they are simultaneously the most powerful and the most confusing experience for both survivors and their partners (Walker, 2013).

Unlike traditional flashbacks, which include visual and sensory memories of a traumatic event, emotional flashbacks involve only feelings. There's no scene, no image, no clear memory of what's happening. The person is suddenly flooded with the overwhelming emotions of childhood trauma: terror, helplessness, shame, abandonment, rage, despair.

Pete Walker, who developed the concept, describes emotional flashbacks as sudden regressions to the feeling states of childhood abuse or neglect. The person's adult self temporarily disappears, and they experience the world through the eyes of the wounded child they once were. They feel small, powerless, and in danger, even when objectively they're safe (Walker, 2013).

What makes emotional flashbacks so difficult is their invisibility. Your partner can't point to what's happening. They may not even recognize that they're having a flashback. They just suddenly feel terrible, and everything in the present moment gets filtered through that awfulness. You become the source of their distress because you're there, even if you did nothing wrong.

4.2 Why There Are No Pictures

The reason emotional flashbacks lack visual content relates to how trauma affects memory, particularly developmental trauma.

Explicit memories, the kind we can consciously recall and describe, require a fully developed hippocampus and the capacity for verbal narrative. Young children don't have this capacity fully online, especially children under extreme stress (van der Kolk, 2014).

What children do encode, powerfully, is implicit memory: body sensations, emotional states, relational patterns. The child may not remember the specific incident of being screamed at, but their body remembers the fear. They may not recall the details of being neglected, but they remember the desolation.

These implicit memories don't announce themselves as memories. They just arise as current experiences. "I feel afraid" not "I remember being afraid." The feeling doesn't come labeled "this is about the past." It just feels true, right now.

This is why your partner may insist they don't have trauma memories. They're not lying. They genuinely may not have visual recall of traumatic events. But their nervous system remembers everything, and when triggered, it responds as if the past is happening now.

4.3 Common Flashback Triggers

Almost anything can trigger an emotional flashback if it resembles, even subtly, something from the original trauma environment. Here are some common triggers that partners inadvertently activate:

Criticism, even gentle or constructive, can trigger shame floods if the original environment was critical. Your partner may hear "Could you load the dishwasher differently?" as "You're worthless and can't do anything right."

Silence or withdrawal during conflict can trigger abandonment terror. If a parent used the silent treatment as punishment, your quietness during an argument may feel like you've disappeared and will never return.

Raised voices or sharp tones, even if not directed at your partner, can activate fear responses. A child who lived with a raging parent learned that loud means danger.

Changes in routine or unexpected events can destabilize a nervous system that survived by hypervigilance. The child who never knew what mood their parent would be in learned to track everything. Unpredictability still feels threatening.

Feeling unseen or dismissed triggers the old wound of neglect. If you're distracted when your partner is talking, they may suddenly feel like they don't exist or don't matter.

Intimacy and vulnerability themselves can be triggers. Being truly close means being truly exposed, and exposure meant danger.

Physical sensations sometimes trigger flashbacks: certain touches, smells, sounds, or even internal states like fatigue or hunger that resemble conditions during the original trauma.

4.4 What Partners See

During an emotional flashback, your partner's behavior changes in ways that may confuse or frighten you. Understanding what you're seeing helps you respond more effectively.

Sudden mood shifts are perhaps the most common indicator. One moment everything is fine, and the next your partner is withdrawn, tearful, angry, or shut down. The shift seems to come from nowhere because, to them, it often does. They may not consciously register the trigger.

Disproportionate reactions are another sign. The response is way bigger than the situation warrants. They're sobbing over a missed call. They're furious about a minor scheduling conflict. They're devastated by a small critique. The intensity makes no sense until you understand they're not reacting to the present. They're reliving the past.

Withdrawal or shutdown happens when the nervous system moves into freeze mode. Your partner may become silent, go blank, or seem to disappear behind their eyes. They're there but not there. This is dissociation, a survival response to overwhelming threat.

Rage that seems to come from nowhere is the fight response activated. Your partner may lash out with anger that doesn't fit the situation. They may become accusatory, defensive, or hostile. This isn't the adult you know; it's a terrified child fighting for survival.

Childlike behavior or speech patterns sometimes emerge during flashbacks. Your partner's voice may change pitch. Their vocabulary may become simpler. Their body language may shift. They may seem literally younger because, in that moment, they are the age they were when the original trauma occurred.

Apollonia described what she observed in her partner Cyril: "It's like watching someone transform. His whole face changes. His shoulders come up. His voice gets tight and high. He'll say things like 'I'm sorry, I'm sorry, please don't' when I haven't done anything. Then an hour later, he's back and has no idea what happened."

4.5 The Amnesia Effect

One of the most painful aspects of emotional flashbacks is the amnesia they create around safety.

Your partner knows you're safe. They've experienced your kindness thousands of times. They trust you, as much as they're capable of trusting anyone. But during a flashback, all of that knowledge becomes temporarily inaccessible.

The brain under threat prioritizes survival over reason. The prefrontal cortex, which holds context and perspective, goes offline. What remains is the survival-focused amygdala, which doesn't do nuance. It knows one thing: danger (van der Kolk, 2014).

During a flashback, your partner may genuinely believe you're going to hurt them, leave them, or betray them. They may treat you like the people who actually did those things. They may forget every positive experience you've shared. This isn't manipulation or choice. It's neurobiological hijacking.

After the flashback passes, they may feel confused and ashamed. They know, intellectually, that you didn't deserve their reaction. But in the moment, they couldn't access that knowing.

This is why repeated reassurance during a flashback often doesn't help. The part of the brain that could receive reassurance isn't online. The words don't register. Or worse, they register as lies because the traumatized brain "knows" that people who say nice things eventually hurt you.

4.6 Duration And Intensity

Emotional flashbacks vary widely in duration and intensity.

Some are brief, lasting minutes. Your partner dips into a triggered state, then surfaces relatively quickly. These may be so subtle that neither of you fully recognizes what happened. There's just a moment of tension, a slightly disproportionate response, and then things normalize.

Others last hours. The flashback sets in and doesn't release. Your partner is stuck in the emotional state, unable to shake it. They may try to function normally while feeling internally devastated.

Some flashbacks persist for days. Walker describes these as extended regressions where the person can't seem to climb out of the pit. Everything feels hopeless, and every interaction reinforces the negative state.

Intensity also varies. A mild flashback might register as irritability, anxiety, or a general sense of things being "off." A severe flashback might involve complete dissociation, uncontrollable sobbing, panic attacks, or rage.

Factors that affect severity include: how closely the trigger resembles the original trauma, your partner's overall stress level, physical factors like fatigue or hunger, whether additional triggers pile up, and how the flashback is responded to by people around them.

4.7 The Dishes That Were Not About The Dishes

Here's a story that illustrates how emotional flashbacks work in daily life.

Nephele and her partner Theophilus had been together for two years. Theophilus had disclosed early on that his childhood was difficult, but he didn't talk about specifics. Nephele knew to be gentle with criticism, but she didn't fully understand why.

One Saturday, she asked Theophilus if he'd remembered to mail the rent check. He hadn't. It was a simple mistake, easily fixed. But before she could say "That's okay, we'll mail it Monday," Theophilus's face crumpled. He started apologizing frantically. He offered to pay any late fees himself. His voice became younger, more desperate. "I'm sorry, I'm so stupid, I always mess things up, I'm sorry."

Nephele was baffled. "It's fine, really, it's just a rent check." But Theophilus couldn't hear her. He spent the next hour in misery, berating himself, expecting her to leave him over this minor thing.

What Nephele eventually came to understand was this: Theophilus's mother had been ruthlessly critical. Every mistake, no matter how small, was met with contempt and rage. The message was clear: you are defective, and your defects are unforgivable. When Nephele asked about the rent check, Theophilus wasn't responding to her or to the actual situation. He was responding to twenty years of being told he could never do anything right. The forgotten check was proof, in his triggered mind, of his fundamental worthlessness.

This is what it means to say the flashback "isn't about the dishes" or the rent check or whatever the present-moment trigger was. It's about old pain bleeding through into now.

4.8 Recognizing Flashbacks In Your Partner

Learning to recognize emotional flashbacks as they happen can transform how you respond. Here are signs to watch for:

Physical signs include changes in posture (becoming smaller, shoulders rising, body tensing or collapsing), changes in voice (higher pitch, childlike tone, becoming very quiet), changes in eyes (going blank, becoming very wide, looking unfocused), and changes in breathing (becoming shallow, quick, or held).

Emotional signs include sudden flooding of shame, fear, despair, or rage that doesn't match the situation. The intensity is the clue. If the emotion is way bigger than what's happening, a flashback is likely.

Cognitive signs include confusion about the present moment, difficulty finding words, loss of perspective (everything is terrible, nothing will ever be okay), and temporary loss of knowledge about your relationship (forgetting that you're safe, expecting you to behave like the people who hurt them).

Behavioral signs include the 4F responses we'll explore in detail later: fighting (becoming aggressive, critical, defensive), fleeing (wanting to leave, changing the subject, becoming very busy), freezing (going blank, dissociating, shutting down), or fawning (excessive apologizing, frantically trying to please).

When you recognize these signs, you can name what's happening, either to yourself or gently to your partner: "I think you might be having a flashback." This simple recognition can help both of you step back from the content of the moment and address what's really going on.

4.9 First Aid For Flashbacks

While a comprehensive approach to supporting your partner through flashbacks will come in later chapters, here are some immediate principles:

Stay calm yourself. Your regulated presence is the most powerful tool you have. If you escalate, the flashback intensifies. If you remain steady, you provide an anchor.

Don't try to argue them out of it. Logic doesn't reach the triggered brain. Saying "You're overreacting" or "There's nothing to be afraid of" doesn't help and often makes things worse.

Don't take it personally. What your partner is saying or doing right now is about the past, not about you. Remind yourself: this is a flashback.

Speak softly and simply. If you speak at all, use short, simple, reassuring phrases: "You're safe right now. I'm here. This will pass."

Offer grounding gently. If your partner is open to it, help them connect to the present moment: "Can you feel your feet on the floor?

What do you see around you?" But don't force this if they're too activated.

Give space if needed. Some people need physical proximity during flashbacks; others need space. Ask if you can: "Do you want me to stay close or give you some room?"

Wait it out. Flashbacks end. Sometimes all you can do is weather them together and reconnect after.

4.10 After The Storm

When the flashback passes, there's often a vulnerable period. Your partner may feel ashamed, exhausted, confused, or distant. Here's how to navigate this time:

Don't immediately process what happened. Give them time to return fully to the present. Save the analytical conversation for later, if at all.

Offer gentle reconnection. A cup of tea, a quiet "Are you okay?", some casual physical affection if they're receptive. You're rebuilding the bridge between you.

Avoid phrases that minimize. "It wasn't that big a deal" or "See, nothing bad happened" can feel dismissive of what was, for them, very real suffering.

Take care of yourself too. Witnessing flashbacks is hard. You may have your own emotional aftermath to process.

When the time is right, perhaps later that day or another day, you can talk about what happened. What triggered it? What helped? What didn't? This kind of reflection, done gently and with curiosity rather than blame, helps both of you learn to navigate flashbacks more effectively over time.

4.11 Essential Points

Your partner isn't overreacting to the present. They're reliving the past. The emotion is real; it just belongs to an earlier time.

Flashbacks are involuntary, not manipulative. Your partner isn't choosing to have these reactions. Their nervous system is running survival programs without their consent.

Recognition is the first step to helping. When you can name what's happening, you can respond to the flashback rather than getting caught in the content. This changes everything.

Chapter 5.0 The Fight Response in Relationships

Galatea knew Faramond loved her. She had seen his tenderness with their children, his devotion when she was sick, his tears during their wedding vows. But in moments of conflict, that Faramond disappeared. In his place came someone sharp and defensive, someone who attacked before he could be attacked, someone who made her feel like the enemy. "You always do this. You never listen. You're just like my mother." The words cut, and Galatea would find herself defending, apologizing, backing down just to make it stop. Later, Faramond would be remorseful, confused by his own behavior. "I don't know why I get like that. I don't want to hurt you." But it kept happening, until they learned what was underneath: not cruelty, but fear wearing an anger costume.

5.1 The 4F Trauma Typology

Before we go further, let me introduce a framework that will organize much of what follows.

Pete Walker, a therapist and C-PTSD survivor himself, developed what he calls the 4F Trauma Typology. This framework describes four primary survival responses that children develop in response to threatening environments: Fight, Flight, Freeze, and Fawn (Walker, 2013).

These responses are instinctive. All humans have them. They're wired into our neurobiology as ways to survive danger. In healthy development, children learn to use all four responses flexibly, choosing the one that best fits the situation.

In traumatic development, flexibility is lost. The child gravitates toward one or two responses that worked best in their particular environment. These become their default survival strategies. In adulthood, they continue to use these strategies even when they're no longer needed or helpful.

This chapter focuses on the Fight response. Chapters 6 through 8 will address Flight, Freeze, and Fawn, and Chapter 9 will discuss how these types combine.

Understanding your partner's dominant response pattern helps you make sense of their behavior and respond more effectively.

5.2 Fight Explained

The Fight response in trauma is built on an unconscious belief: control creates safety. The Fight type learned that the best defense was a good offense. In their childhood environment, standing ground, pushing back, and dominating the interaction was how they survived.

Some Fight types grew up with parents who respected strength and punished weakness. Only by being tougher than the attacker could they protect themselves. Others discovered that going on offense distracted from their vulnerability. If they could control the situation, maybe they wouldn't be hurt.

In adulthood, the Fight response manifests as aggression, criticism, anger, and the need for control. Fight types may be quick to argue, prone to finding fault, and uncomfortable with vulnerability. They may intimidate others without intending to. They may have difficulty accepting help because needing help feels like weakness (Walker, 2013).

It's important to understand that Fight is a fear response, not a strength. Underneath the aggression is terror. The Fight type learned to convert fear into anger because anger feels more powerful than powerlessness. But the fear is still there, driving everything.

5.3 How Fight Affects Your Relationship

If your partner has a dominant Fight response, you may experience some or all of the following patterns:

Arguments escalate rapidly. What starts as a minor disagreement becomes a major conflict within moments. Your partner goes from zero to sixty before you've registered there's a problem. You may feel blindsided by the intensity.

Criticism feels disproportionate. Your partner notices what's wrong and points it out, often harshly. You may feel you can't do anything right. Even your attempts to please are met with fault-finding.

There's a need to be right or in control. Your partner struggles to let things go, concede a point, or allow decisions to be made without their input. Compromise feels like defeat to them.

Difficulty accepting help or vulnerability. Your partner may resist support, react defensively to expressions of concern, or shut down emotionally. Needing anything feels dangerous.

Blaming is common. When things go wrong, your partner looks for someone to hold responsible, and that someone is often you. Taking accountability is threatening because being "wrong" was dangerous in their childhood.

Darian's partner Berenice put it this way: "Living with Darian was like living with someone who was always ready for battle. Every conversation felt like a potential war zone. I never knew what would set him off. I started to believe I really was the problem, that I really was causing all these conflicts. It took a long time to understand that his anger wasn't really about me at all."

5.4 Fear Beneath The Anger

The Fight response is often the hardest for partners to have compassion for. It's easier to feel sympathetic toward someone who cowers than someone who attacks. But Fight types need compassion too, perhaps especially so.

45

Behind every Fight reaction is fear. Fear of being controlled or dominated. Fear of being vulnerable and therefore hurt. Fear of being seen as weak. Fear of returning to the helplessness of childhood.

When your partner lashes out, they're not showing strength. They're showing how frightened they are. The anger is armor. The criticism is preemptive defense. The control is an attempt to create the safety they never had.

This doesn't excuse harmful behavior. Aggression hurts regardless of its origins, and you have the right to protect yourself. But understanding the fear beneath the anger helps you see your partner more accurately. They're not a bully. They're a wounded person who learned that attacking first was the only way to survive.

5.5 Healthy Assertion Versus Trauma Driven Fight

It's important to distinguish between healthy assertiveness and trauma-driven Fight.

Healthy assertiveness involves stating your needs, setting boundaries, expressing disagreement, and standing up for yourself when appropriate. This is a good thing. Everyone needs to be able to do this.

Trauma-driven Fight goes beyond assertion into aggression. The response is disproportionate to the situation. It's triggered by perceived rather than actual threats. It seeks to dominate or control rather than simply express. And it often causes harm that the person later regrets.

Some signs that Fight behavior is trauma-driven:

The intensity doesn't match the situation. Getting mildly annoyed over a forgotten errand is normal. Raging about it is Fight response.

There's a pattern of regret afterward. Your partner often apologizes or feels bad about how they acted.

The behavior seems involuntary. They describe "seeing red" or not being able to stop themselves.

It's triggered by situations involving vulnerability, criticism, or loss of control. These are the specific threats that activate childhood survival responses.

Historical context connects. Their behavior echoes how they were treated or how they needed to act in their family of origin.

5.6 The Deepest Fear

For Fight types, the deepest fear is being controlled or helpless again.

In childhood, they survived by taking control, by being tough, by refusing to be dominated. That strategy worked then. The problem is that it's still running now, even when it's not needed.

When your partner perceives any threat to their autonomy, any hint that someone might control them or put them in a vulnerable position, the Fight response activates. They attack to prevent what they fear: becoming powerless like they once were.

This is why feedback triggers such intense reactions. Feedback implies that someone else is in a position to evaluate them. This is threatening.

This is why help is rejected. Accepting help means admitting need, which feels like weakness.

This is why intimacy can be difficult. True closeness requires vulnerability, and vulnerability feels dangerous.

Understanding this deepest fear helps you navigate the minefield. When you can see that your partner's anger is really terror, you can respond to the terror rather than the anger.

5.7 What You Might Be Feeling

If your partner has a dominant Fight response, you may be experiencing:

Feeling attacked, even when you've done nothing wrong. Their criticism and anger land on you whether you deserve it or not.

Walking on eggshells, constantly monitoring their mood and trying to avoid setting them off. This is exhausting.

Defensive posture, always preparing to be blamed or criticized. You may have started fighting back, creating escalating conflicts.

Confusion about what you're doing wrong. If only you could get it right, maybe the conflict would stop. (Spoiler: it's not about what you're doing.)

Loss of voice. You may have stopped expressing your own needs or feelings because it seems to make things worse.

Grief for the partner you glimpse between conflicts. You know they're capable of kindness because you've seen it. The contrast with the fighting is painful.

These feelings are valid. You're experiencing the impact of your partner's trauma response, and that impact is real.

5.8 What Is Actually Happening

When your partner's Fight response is activated, their nervous system has perceived a threat and is responding with the strategy that once kept them safe.

This happens faster than conscious thought. The amygdala, the brain's threat-detection center, triggers the survival response in milliseconds. By the time the prefrontal cortex catches up, the reaction is already underway (LeDoux, 2015).

Your partner's perception of threat may have no connection to your actual behavior. You might have said something that triggered an association to their past. You might have looked at them in a way that resembled how someone else looked at them. You might have done absolutely nothing, and they're reacting to an internal state.

Once the Fight response is activated, your partner loses access to nuance, context, and relationship history. They're not choosing to forget that you're safe; the information is simply unavailable to them. They're operating from a part of the brain that doesn't do complexity.

This doesn't make their behavior acceptable. It does explain why rational conversation doesn't work in those moments.

5.9 Responding To The Fight Response

When your partner's Fight response is activated, your own responses matter. Here are some strategies:

Don't take the bait. Fight types often provoke, consciously or not, to keep the battle going. If you escalate with them, you confirm their expectation of conflict and prolong the episode. This doesn't mean being passive or accepting abuse. It means not matching their energy.

Stay grounded in your own body. When someone is aggressive, it's natural to feel your own fight response activate. Notice this. Take a breath. You can choose not to escalate even if your nervous system wants to.

Create safety without surrendering. You don't have to agree with everything they say or back down from all positions. But you can speak calmly, acknowledge their feelings, and refuse to participate in warfare. "I hear that you're really upset. I want to talk about this, and I need us to be calmer to do that."

Set clear limits. "I'm not going to continue this conversation while you're yelling at me. I'll be in the other room when you're ready to talk differently." Then follow through.

Wait for regulation before addressing content. The issue that triggered the fight can be discussed later, when both of you are calm. Trying to resolve problems during activation makes everything worse.

Know when to walk away. If your safety is threatened, leave. This is non-negotiable. Fight responses can sometimes become dangerous, and your wellbeing matters.

5.10 After The Fight

After the intensity passes, there's often a window for repair. This is crucial. How you navigate the aftermath affects whether the relationship heals or erodes.

Give time for full regulation. Don't rush into processing. Your partner may need hours or even a day to fully come back to baseline.

Name what happened without blame. "I think that was a flashback" or "That felt like old stuff coming up" can help create shared understanding without making your partner feel attacked again.

Express your experience without attacking. "I felt really scared when you were yelling. I know you weren't trying to hurt me, and it still affected me."

Make room for their experience too. Your partner probably feels shame about their behavior. They may need to talk about what triggered them. Listening with curiosity helps.

Reconnect before rehashing. Sometimes a hug, a cup of tea, or doing something ordinary together is more healing than immediate conversation.

Discuss preventive strategies when you're both calm. "What could help next time? Is there a signal we could use? What do you need from me when you're starting to feel that way?"

5.11 When Fight Becomes Abuse

There's a line between trauma-driven aggression and abuse, and that line matters.

Occasional angry outbursts that your partner regrets, understands as problematic, and is working to change are one thing. Ongoing patterns of intimidation, control, threats, or violence are something else entirely.

Red flags that suggest abuse rather than trauma response:

The behavior is targeted and controlled. They can turn it off in public or around certain people, which means they can control it.

There's no remorse or accountability. They blame you entirely and never acknowledge their role.

The pattern escalates over time rather than improving with awareness.

Physical safety is threatened. Any violence or threats of violence cross the line.

You feel increasingly trapped, isolated, or afraid.

Having C-PTSD does not excuse abuse. Many trauma survivors never become abusers. If your partner's behavior has crossed into abuse territory, please seek support. Chapter 24 addresses when staying is no longer advisable.

5.12 Key Principles

Fight is a fear response wearing an anger costume. Your partner's aggression isn't about power; it's about terror.

Your partner isn't trying to hurt you. They're trying not to be hurt. The attacks are defensive, not offensive.

Boundaries are essential, not optional. Compassion for your partner's trauma doesn't mean accepting harmful behavior. You can understand and still protect yourself.

Chapter 6.0 The Flight Response in Relationships

Salome fell in love with Marius's ambition. He was driven, successful, always working toward the next goal. She admired his energy, his commitment, his ability to get things done. It took two years before she noticed she was always alone. Marius was there in body, but his attention was on his phone, his projects, his perpetual to-do list. Date nights became work dinners. Weekends disappeared into "just one more thing." When she asked him to slow down, he agreed but nothing changed. When she cried, he seemed confused. "I'm doing this for us," he insisted. But us was disappearing, and Marius couldn't seem to stop running long enough to notice.

6.1 Flight Explained

The Flight response in trauma is built on an unconscious belief: if I stay busy enough, the feelings can't catch me.

Flight types learned in childhood that escaping was the way to survive. This escape might have been literal (leaving the house, staying at friends' homes, disappearing into activities) or psychological (escaping into achievement, fantasy, or distraction). The key insight they developed was that stillness was dangerous. When they stopped moving, the pain caught up.

In adulthood, the Flight response manifests as workaholism, perfectionism, constant activity, and an inability to simply be. Flight types are always doing. They're anxious when plans fall through. They fill every moment with tasks, goals, or stimulation. They may be highly successful by external measures because all that energy goes somewhere (Walker, 2013).

The cost, especially in relationships, is that they're never truly present. Their bodies are there, but their attention is elsewhere.

Intimacy requires slowing down, and slowing down feels threatening.

6.2 How Flight Affects Your Relationship

If your partner has a dominant Flight response, you may experience some or all of the following patterns:

Emotional unavailability despite physical presence. Your partner is home, but they're working on the laptop, scrolling their phone, mentally elsewhere. You feel like you're competing with their to-do list.

Difficulty relaxing or just being together. Downtime makes them anxious. They suggest activities, find projects, or seem uncomfortable with unstructured time.

Prioritizing work or hobbies over connection. There's always something more urgent than the relationship. Deadlines, obligations, goals take precedence over quality time.

Anxiety when plans change. Flight types often manage their anxiety through structure and busyness. Unexpected free time feels threatening.

Obsessive exercise, hobbies, or productivity. What looks like healthy dedication might actually be compulsive escape. The gym, the garden, the home improvement projects become hiding places.

Resistance to slowing down even when burned out. They push through exhaustion rather than rest because resting means feeling.

Ivo described his experience with his partner Eudora: "She was always on the go. I thought at first it was just who she was. Then I noticed she literally couldn't sit still. If we had a quiet evening planned, she'd find something that urgently needed doing. Movie nights became her folding laundry while half-watching the screen. I started to feel like a burden, like spending time with me wasn't worth stopping for."

6.3 Success That Feels Like Abandonment

One of the painful paradoxes of loving a Flight type is that their survival strategy often looks like success.

Your partner may be high-achieving, admired, accomplished. They may provide well, earn promotions, complete impressive projects. From the outside, everything looks great.

From the inside, you feel abandoned. All that energy goes everywhere except into the relationship. You're proud of them and lonely at the same time.

This creates a confusing situation where it feels wrong to complain. How can you resent someone for being hardworking? How can you ask them to be less successful? You might even be benefiting from their achievements, financially or in terms of social status.

But the emotional cost is real. A relationship requires presence. You can't feel loved by someone who isn't there, however good their reasons for absence. And your partner's reasons, while framed as noble (providing for the family, building a career, completing important work), are actually driven by the need to avoid their own internal experience.

This isn't selfish in the usual sense. They're not choosing work over you consciously. They're running from feelings that feel unsurvivable. You're just collateral damage.

6.4 The Deepest Fear

For Flight types, the deepest fear is stillness and the feelings it brings.

In childhood, stopping meant being present to pain. When they slowed down, the emotions caught up: the fear, the grief, the loneliness, the inadequacy. Busyness became the solution. As long as they were moving, they didn't have to feel.

This pattern continues in adulthood. Your partner may not even be aware that they're fleeing. They think they just have a strong work ethic, that they're naturally high-energy, that they enjoy being productive. The underlying terror is often unconscious.

But put them in a situation where they can't be busy, where they're forced to sit with their feelings or with intimate connection, and the anxiety emerges. They become restless, irritable, or find reasons why they need to be doing something.

Understanding this fear helps you see your partner's behavior differently. When they can't put down their phone, they're not disrespecting you. They're desperately avoiding something inside themselves. When they can't take a vacation, they're not choosing work over you. They're afraid of what happens when the distractions stop.

6.5 What You Might Be Feeling

If your partner has a dominant Flight response, you may be experiencing:

Loneliness in the relationship. You're partnered but feel like you're doing life alone. This is an especially confusing kind of loneliness.

Feeling like you're second to their work or activities. Their priorities, in action if not in words, seem to place you below their to-do list.

Questioning whether you matter to them. If they really loved you, wouldn't they want to spend time with you?

Resentment building. You may have tried to accept their busyness but find yourself increasingly angry about it.

Minimizing your own needs. You might tell yourself you're being needy or that other people have real problems. This keeps you from advocating for what you need.

Exhaustion from trying to match their pace. Some partners try to keep up with Flight types, becoming busy themselves just to spend time together.

6.6 What Is Actually Happening

When your partner's Flight response is operating, they're driven by anxiety that they may not even recognize as anxiety.

The nervous system of a Flight type is calibrated for constant movement. Dopamine hits from accomplishment and the structure of busyness create a sense of safety, even if it's illusory. Stillness triggers the opposite: a sense of undefined dread (Porges, 2011).

Your partner isn't consciously rejecting you. They're managing their internal state in the only way they know how. The tragedy is that the very thing that could help them most (relational presence, safe connection) is the thing they can't access because it requires the stillness they fear.

They may also be running from intimacy specifically. Getting too close to you means getting too vulnerable. Busyness creates distance, which feels safer than the exposure that love requires.

6.7 Responding To The Flight Response

Working with a Flight partner requires creativity and patience. Here are some strategies:

Join them in activity rather than demanding stillness. If they can't sit and talk, walk and talk. If they're anxious doing nothing, do something together. Connection during activity may be more achievable than connection during rest.

Suggest structured time. Flight types often do better with scheduled intimacy than spontaneous demands for presence. "Can we have dinner together from 6 to 7 with no phones?" gives them a container that feels manageable.

Take small bites. Instead of asking for a whole unplugged weekend, ask for one hour. Build gradually.

Name the pattern gently. "I notice we don't have much unstructured time together" opens conversation without attacking.

Express what you need without attacking who they are. "I need more of your presence" rather than "You're a workaholic who doesn't care about me."

Celebrate moments of presence. When they do slow down, acknowledge it. Positive reinforcement helps reshape patterns.

Address your own needs independently as well. This isn't about giving up on connection. But having your own fulfillment outside the relationship takes pressure off and models that stillness doesn't have to be lonely.

6.8 Helping Them Build Capacity

Flight types often don't know how to just be. This isn't a moral failing; it's a skill they never developed because their childhood required constant movement.

You can help them build capacity for presence, slowly and gently:

Start with short periods. Five minutes of sitting together without devices or distractions. Let them build tolerance.

Use grounding activities. Things like breathing exercises, gentle stretching, or mindfulness practices can help regulate the anxious energy that drives Flight. Doing these together normalizes them.

Create rituals of connection. Morning coffee without phones. Evening check-ins. Small, predictable moments of togetherness that become expected rather than threatening.

Be patient with setbacks. They will fall back into busyness, especially when stressed. This isn't failure; it's the nature of ingrained patterns.

Encourage their own work on this in therapy. Flight is a survival adaptation, and deeply changing it usually requires professional support.

Clotilde found that cooking with her partner Aurelian worked better than trying to get him to watch movies. "He couldn't just sit, but he could chop vegetables. We'd prep dinner together and talk. It wasn't cuddling on the couch, but we were together, and he was actually present. Later, we worked up to quieter time, but we had to start where he could succeed."

6.9 When Flight Masks Depression

Sometimes Flight behavior masks underlying depression. The constant activity keeps the person one step ahead of despair. If they stop, they crash.

Signs that depression may be involved:

Complete collapse when busyness is enforced to stop (illness, job loss, vacation where activities aren't possible)

Sleep as an alternate escape (extreme busyness followed by oversleeping)

Lack of joy in the activities despite doing so many of them

Existential emptiness expressed when they do slow down

If you notice these patterns, professional help is important. Flight as a defense against depression is particularly exhausting and can lead to burnout.

6.10 Key Principles

Busyness is a form of avoidance, not rejection of you. Your partner isn't choosing work over you; they're running from their own inner experience.

Your partner may not know how to simply be in relationship. The stillness required for intimacy is a skill they never learned.

Patience and creativity can build connection over time. Meeting them where they are, slowly building capacity for presence, and recognizing progress all help.

Chapter 7.0 The Freeze Response in Relationships

The first few months with Benedictus, Jessamine felt chosen. He was quiet, attentive, focused entirely on her when they were together. She interpreted his stillness as calm, his silence as depth. It wasn't until they moved in together that she saw the other side of his quietness. Conflict arose, as it does, and Benedictus simply... disappeared. Not physically, but entirely. His eyes went blank. His responses became monosyllabic. He retreated to his computer for hours, seemingly deaf to her attempts to reach him. She'd knock on the study door, and he'd look up like he didn't recognize her. "I just need some space," he'd say, and then the space stretched into days. Jessamine started to wonder if she was living with a ghost.

7.1 Freeze Explained

The Freeze response in trauma is built on an unconscious belief: if I'm invisible, I can't be hurt.

Freeze types learned in childhood that hiding was the safest option. They couldn't fight back effectively. They couldn't run away. What they could do was become small, quiet, and unnoticed. By disappearing, they avoided drawing the dangerous attention of their caregivers.

In adulthood, the Freeze response manifests as isolation, dissociation, withdrawal, and what can look like depression. Freeze types may spend excessive time alone, avoid social situations, struggle to take initiative, and seem emotionally absent even when physically present. They're the "lost children," the ones who escaped notice by never being truly there (Walker, 2013).

This is perhaps the most misunderstood of the 4F responses because it can be mistaken for laziness, apathy, or lack of love. In reality,

Freeze is a survival state of profound overwhelm where the nervous system has essentially shut down.

7.2 How Freeze Affects Your Relationship

If your partner has a dominant Freeze response, you may experience some or all of the following patterns:

Emotional shutdown during conflict. When disagreements arise, your partner becomes unreachable. They may still be talking, but there's no one home behind the words.

Physical withdrawal. They retreat to other rooms, sleep excessively, or disappear into screens. The physical distance mirrors the emotional unavailability.

Difficulty initiating. They struggle to start conversations, make plans, or take action. They seem to be waiting for something but can't say what.

Seeming checked out or unreachable. Even during good times, there's a quality of absence. You find yourself working hard to draw them out.

Dissociation during intimacy or important conversations. At the moments when connection matters most, they fade away. Sex may feel like they're not really there. Deep conversations lose them.

Low energy and motivation that resembles depression. The overall impression is of someone who is barely engaged with life.

Dorothea described her experience with her partner Osric: "It was like loving someone through a pane of glass. I could see him, but I couldn't touch him. When I needed him most, he was gone, even when he was sitting right in front of me. The loneliest I've ever felt was in the same room with someone who wasn't really there."

7.3 Understanding Dissociation

Dissociation is a core feature of the Freeze response, and understanding it helps make sense of your partner's behavior.

Dissociation is a disconnection between normally integrated aspects of experience: thoughts, feelings, sensations, memories, identity. It exists on a spectrum from mild (daydreaming, highway hypnosis) to severe (complete loss of time, alternate identities). Most people with C-PTSD experience dissociation somewhere in the middle (van der Kolk, 2014).

Common dissociative experiences include:

Depersonalization. Feeling detached from one's own body or mental processes. Your partner may describe feeling like they're watching themselves from outside, or like they're not real.

Derealization. Feeling like the world around them isn't real. Things may seem foggy, dreamlike, or two-dimensional.

Emotional numbing. Feeling nothing when they "should" feel something. The ability to access emotions is cut off.

Memory gaps. Not remembering periods of time, especially stressful times. Your partner may not recall conversations or events that you clearly remember.

Identity confusion. Uncertainty about who they are, shifting sense of self, or feeling like different people at different times.

Dissociation is a survival response. When threat is unavoidable and overwhelming, the mind escapes even when the body can't. It's a form of self-protection. But in adulthood, when it's triggered by situations that aren't actually dangerous, it creates disconnection from life and from relationships.

7.4 The Deepest Fear

For Freeze types, the deepest fear is that engagement brings annihilation.

In childhood, being noticed meant being hurt. The child learned that visibility was dangerous. Better to be invisible, to not exist, than to draw the attention that led to pain.

This belief persists unconsciously in adulthood. Your partner may not think "If I engage, I'll be destroyed." But their nervous system acts as though this is true. Retreating into dissociation, hiding in isolation, disappearing into screens or sleep are all ways of becoming invisible again.

Intimacy is especially threatening because it requires being seen. Really being seen by a loving partner, in all one's vulnerability. For someone whose developmental experience was that being seen led to being hurt, this feels like existential danger.

Your partner may genuinely want connection. They may love you deeply. But the moment real closeness becomes possible, the Freeze response activates and they vanish.

7.5 What You Might Be Feeling

If your partner has a dominant Freeze response, you may be experiencing:

Profound loneliness in the relationship. You have a partner who isn't really there. This is a particular kind of isolation.

Frustration at not being able to reach them. You try everything, and nothing seems to bring them back. The wall is impenetrable.

Feeling invisible yourself. If they can't really see you, do you even exist?

Grief for the relationship you imagined. You fell in love with someone who seemed more present at the beginning. Where did that person go?

Exhaustion from carrying the relational load. You're doing all the emotional labor because they're not capable of meeting you halfway.

Confusion about whether they love you. Their absence feels like indifference, even though you suspect it's something else.

7.6 What Is Actually Happening

When your partner is in Freeze, their nervous system has moved into a state that Stephen Porges calls dorsal vagal shutdown. This is the most primitive survival response, essentially playing dead. Metabolic activity decreases, engagement with the environment ceases, and the person may appear depressed, checked out, or barely alive (Porges, 2011).

This is not a choice. Your partner isn't choosing to withdraw from you any more than someone fainting is choosing to lose consciousness. The nervous system has determined that the threat level is too high for fight or flight, and it has implemented the last-ditch survival option: collapse.

The threat triggering this response may have nothing to do with you. It may be triggered by stress at work, conflict (which they perceive as more dangerous than it is), intimacy itself, or internal states they're not even aware of.

What you see from the outside (withdrawal, absence, shutdown) is the visible manifestation of an internal state of profound overwhelm. Your partner is, in a sense, not there because being fully present feels unsurvivable.

7.7 Responding To The Freeze Response

Working with a Freeze partner requires gentleness and patience. Here are some strategies:

Offer gentle, non-demanding presence. Sometimes the best thing you can do is simply be nearby without requiring anything from them. Sitting in the same room, doing your own thing, not pressuring them to engage, creates a sense of safety.

Respect their need for solitude while maintaining a connection thread. They may need to retreat, and that's okay. But maintain small points of contact: a text saying you love them, a cup of tea left outside the door. The message is: I'm here when you're ready.

Make small bids for engagement without pressure. "Would you like to take a short walk?" "Want to sit with me for five minutes?" If they say no, accept it gracefully and try again later.

Avoid overwhelming them with intensity. Big emotional conversations, demands for immediate engagement, expressions of frustration about their withdrawal, these can push them further into Freeze. Slow and gentle works better.

Learn their warning signs. Often there are cues that a Freeze state is coming: certain facial expressions, posture changes, voice going flat. If you can recognize these early, you might be able to help them stay connected.

Help with basic functioning if needed. During severe Freeze states, basic tasks become overwhelming. Without becoming their caretaker, gentle help with practical matters can ease the load.

7.8 When To Seek Professional Help

Freeze responses can be particularly debilitating and are closely associated with depression and severe dissociative disorders. There are times when professional help is essential:

If your partner has significant gaps in memory or reports feeling like they "lose time."

If the Freeze state is persistent and prevents normal functioning (can't go to work, can't take care of basic needs).

If there are any signs of suicidal thoughts. Severe depression and dissociation increase suicide risk.

If your own wellbeing is significantly compromised by trying to support them through frequent or prolonged Freeze episodes.

Freeze patterns often require therapeutic support to address effectively. The underlying trauma needs to be processed in a safe environment, and the nervous system needs to learn that engagement can be safe.

7.9 Reaching The Frozen Partner

There's hope in understanding that underneath the Freeze, your partner is still there. They haven't stopped loving you. They've been overwhelmed by survival responses that take them away.

Recovery from Freeze patterns is possible. It requires learning that presence is safe, that engagement doesn't lead to destruction, that they can come out of hiding and survive. This learning happens slowly, through repeated experiences of safe connection.

Your steady, patient presence is part of that learning. Every time you stay calm when they withdraw, every time you welcome them back without punishment when they return, every time you demonstrate that closeness doesn't have to hurt, you're contributing to their nervous system's re-education.

This is long, slow work. There will be setbacks. Your partner may seem to make progress and then disappear again. This is normal. Nervous system patterns change gradually, not all at once.

7.10 Key Principles

Freeze is not laziness or lack of love. It's profound overwhelm. Your partner's withdrawal is a survival response, not a rejection of you.

Your partner may be fighting to come back to you. Inside the Freeze, there's often a part of them that desperately wants connection but can't access it.

Patience and gentle consistency can slowly bring them present. Safe experiences, repeated over time, teach the nervous system that it's okay to engage.

Chapter 8.0 The Fawn Response in Relationships

Everything Ianthe wanted, Simeon provided. Her favorite coffee, waiting when she woke. Her preferences anticipated before she voiced them. Her moods tracked and responded to with precision. At first, it felt like being adored. Later, it started to feel unsettling. "What do you want for dinner?" she'd ask. "Whatever you want," Simeon would answer. "What do you think about this decision?" "Whatever you think is best." "Are you happy?" "If you're happy." It was like loving a mirror, a reflection that gave back only what she projected, with no substance of its own underneath. When Ianthe finally said, "But who are you?" Simeon looked terrified. He genuinely didn't know.

8.1 Fawn Explained

The Fawn response in trauma is built on an unconscious belief: my needs don't matter; your happiness is my safety.

Fawn types learned in childhood that the way to survive was to please the dangerous caregiver. By anticipating needs, agreeing with everything, and making themselves useful, they could sometimes avoid harm. Their strategy was to become whatever the other person wanted them to be.

In adulthood, the Fawn response manifests as people-pleasing, codependency, loss of self, and difficulty with boundaries. Fawn types merge with others, taking on their partners' opinions, preferences, and emotions. They struggle to identify their own wants and needs because they've spent a lifetime suppressing them (Walker, 2013).

This is the most recently recognized of the 4F responses, and it's particularly common in relationships because it looks, at first, like ideal partnership. The Fawn type is accommodating, agreeable, and focused entirely on making their partner happy. It takes time to recognize the problem: there's no actual person there to be in relationship with.

8.2 How Fawn Affects Your Relationship

If your partner has a dominant Fawn response, you may experience some or all of the following patterns:

Agreement with everything, even when it's not authentic. Your partner goes along with whatever you want, rarely expressing preferences or opinions of their own.

Difficulty expressing needs or preferences. When you ask what they want, they genuinely don't know. Or they say what they think you want to hear.

Over-apologizing. They say sorry constantly, even for things that don't require apology, even for existing.

Anticipating your needs before you know them yourself. This can feel loving, but it can also feel like surveillance. How do they know what you want before you do?

Inability to say no. They take on more than they can handle, agree to things that don't serve them, and resent it later without expressing the resentment directly.

Losing identity within the relationship. Over time, they seem to have fewer of their own interests, friends, or opinions. Their whole self becomes organized around you.

Aurelian described his confusion about his partner Melisande: "At first I thought I'd found someone who just really loved to take care of me. Then I realized she took care of everyone like that. She didn't have any preferences, any self. I couldn't figure out who I was actually dating. She was whoever she thought I wanted her to be, which meant I was essentially in a relationship with my own projections."

8.3 The Perfect Partner Problem

The Fawn response is particularly insidious because it mimics what many people think they want in a relationship.

A partner who always agrees? Who puts your needs first? Who never makes demands? Who's always accommodating? This sounds ideal on the surface.

The problem is that real relationships require two whole people. Intimacy means knowing and being known. If your partner has no self to offer, no boundaries to respect, no desires of their own, there's no one there to be intimate with.

You may start to feel lonely even though your partner is constantly attending to you. You may feel guilty for having needs because they never seem to have any. You may feel like you're being suffocated by attention or that you're always taking without giving because they won't let you give.

You may also start to feel manipulated, even though that's not quite what's happening. Fawn types aren't consciously manipulating; they're surviving. But the effect can feel similar: you're never sure what they really think or feel, so you can't trust what they tell you.

8.4 The Deepest Fear

For Fawn types, the deepest fear is that having needs leads to abandonment.

In childhood, having needs was dangerous. The child learned that their wants didn't matter, that expressing them led to rejection or punishment, and that the only way to maintain connection was to suppress the self entirely. They became whatever was needed, a chameleon who survived by having no true form.

This belief persists into adulthood. Your partner fears, at a deep level, that if they show you who they really are, you'll leave. If they disagree with you, you'll reject them. If they have needs, you'll be burdened and abandon them. The only safe strategy is to have no self that could be rejected.

The irony is painful. By hiding themselves to prevent abandonment, they make genuine intimacy impossible. And genuine intimacy is what they actually crave.

8.5 What You Might Be Feeling

If your partner has a dominant Fawn response, you may be experiencing:

Confusion about who your partner really is. You've been together for months or years, and you still don't know their actual preferences.

Guilt for having needs when they don't seem to have any. The imbalance makes you feel like you're taking advantage, even though you're not.

Frustration with lack of authenticity. You want to know what they really think, and they keep giving you what they think you want to hear.

Pressure to be perfect. Since they're tracking your every mood and trying to please you, you may feel you can't have bad days without it becoming their crisis.

Loneliness from not being truly known. They're so focused on pleasing you that they don't really see you either.

Concern that they're not okay. Under all that pleasing, something is clearly wrong. But they won't let you in to help.

8.6 What Is Actually Happening

The Fawn response is a survival strategy of merging with the perceived source of threat (or source of needed attachment).

Your partner's nervous system learned that autonomy was dangerous. Having a separate self, with separate needs, led to punishment, rejection, or simply not getting the connection they needed to survive. The solution was to become an extension of the caregiver, with no independent existence (Walker, 2013).

In your relationship, this pattern continues. Your partner isn't choosing to have no preferences; they genuinely may not have access to their own internal states. Years of suppression have disconnected them from their own wants and needs.

They're not trying to manipulate you by being agreeable. They're trying to be safe. The strategy that once kept them alive in a dangerous household is now operating automatically in a situation that doesn't require it.

8.7 Responding To The Fawn Response

Working with a Fawn partner requires encouraging authenticity while recognizing how frightening that is for them. Here are some strategies:

Create safety for disagreement. Explicitly invite differing opinions. "I really want to know what you think, even if it's different from what I think." "It's okay to disagree with me." Then, crucially, respond well when they do.

Celebrate when they say no. If they manage to express a boundary or decline something, acknowledge it positively. "I'm glad you told me that." This is a big deal for them.

Ask open-ended questions and tolerate "I don't know." "What would you like to do?" may be met with uncertainty. That's okay. Give them time and space to find themselves. Avoid immediately filling in the blank.

Model healthy self-advocacy. Show them what it looks like to have needs, express preferences, and set boundaries without the world ending. Your example teaches them that having a self is survivable.

Resist the urge to take advantage of their pleasing. It would be easy to let them do everything for you since they seem to want to. Don't. This reinforces the pattern.

Point out the pattern gently. "I notice you often say whatever you think I want. I'd really like to know what you actually think." Name the dynamic without shaming them for it.

8.8 Helping Them Find Themselves

Fawn types often have genuinely underdeveloped sense of self. They may not be withholding who they are; they may not know who they are.

Recovery involves reconnecting with their own internal experience, learning to identify wants, needs, feelings, and preferences that have been suppressed for so long they're unfamiliar.

This is delicate work, usually requiring therapy. But you can support it:

Ask about small preferences. "Do you want tea or coffee?" is less threatening than "What do you want from life?" Start small.

Notice what seems to light them up. They may show enthusiasm or preferences before the Fawn reflex kicks in and suppresses them. Catch those moments.

Encourage separate activities and interests. Time apart where they can develop their own sense of self is healthy. They don't have to be merged with you at all times.

Be patient. A lifetime of self-suppression doesn't reverse quickly. There will be many moments where they default back to "whatever you want." This is a long process.

Nephele found that giving her partner Theophilus specific choices helped: "Instead of 'What do you want for dinner?' which paralyzed him, I'd say 'I'm thinking either pasta or tacos, which sounds better to you?' Narrowing it down made it possible for him to actually choose. We built from there."

8.9 The Hidden Resentment

One thing to be aware of with Fawn partners: the suppressed needs don't disappear. They go underground.

Fawn types often develop significant resentment over time because they're constantly giving while their own needs go unmet. They may not express this resentment directly (that would be having needs), so it comes out sideways: passive aggression, withdrawal, sudden explosions, or chronic health problems that may have an emotional component.

If your partner seems to be holding back anger or resentment, gently create space for it. "I wonder if part of you is angry about always putting my needs first." Giving permission for the resentment to exist is part of giving permission for them to exist.

8.10 Key Principles

Fawning isn't love. It's survival wearing love's costume. Your partner's pleasing behavior isn't about how much they love you; it's about how unsafe they feel.

Your partner needs permission to have a self. They learned that selfhood was dangerous. Your acceptance of their authentic person, preferences and all, helps heal that wound.

True intimacy requires two whole people. The relationship can only go as deep as both people are willing to show up as themselves.

Chapter 9.0 Hybrid Types and Shifts

Galatea had thought she understood her partner Darian. He was a Fight type, quick to anger, defensive, controlling. She'd learned to navigate his sharp edges. Then one week, everything changed. Instead of fighting, he collapsed. Slept for sixteen hours, couldn't get off the couch, barely spoke. Where did the angry man go? A month later, he was back to fighting, and Galatea felt like she was partnered with multiple different people. "I don't know which version of you I'm going to get," she told him. "Neither do I," he admitted.

9.1 Pure Types Are Rare

While the previous chapters described each 4F response as if it were a distinct category, the reality is more complex.

Most people with C-PTSD aren't pure types. They're hybrids, with a primary response and one or more secondary responses that emerge under certain conditions. Or they shift between responses depending on context, stress level, or what's being triggered (Walker, 2013).

This is important to understand because it explains why your partner may seem like different people at different times. It's not that they're deliberately confusing you. Their nervous system has multiple survival strategies, and different situations call forth different responses.

9.2 Common Hybrid Combinations

Certain combinations appear frequently:

Fight-Flight is common. This person is the angry workaholic, someone who's always busy and becomes aggressive when that busyness is interrupted or when they're forced into vulnerability. They attack and then escape into activity. They may be highly successful and highly difficult to live with.

77

Flight-Freeze appears in people who are constantly busy until they crash. They run and run and run, and then collapse completely. The cycle of productivity followed by depression or withdrawal can be confusing for partners who see both the go-getter and the checked-out person.

Freeze-Fawn combines withdrawal with people-pleasing. This person may seem passive and accommodating while also being absent and dissociated. They merge with others while not really being present. It's like living with a pleasant ghost.

Fight-Fawn creates someone who alternates between aggression and submission. They may be controlling and critical, then suddenly become excessively apologetic and pleasing when they fear they've gone too far. The whiplash between dominating and submitting is disorienting.

Your partner's particular combination is unique to their history and temperament. The important thing is to recognize that multiple patterns can coexist.

9.3 How Stress Affects Response

One key factor in which response emerges is the overall stress level.

Under moderate stress, your partner's primary type usually dominates. If they're a Fight type, they become more critical and controlling. If they're Flight, they become busier. If they're Freeze, they become more withdrawn. If they're Fawn, they become more accommodating.

Under severe stress, or when the primary response fails, they may shift to a secondary type. The Fight type who can't win the battle may collapse into Freeze. The Flight type who's forced to stop running may shift into Fight or Freeze. The Fawn type whose pleasing isn't working may become aggressive.

Under extreme or prolonged stress, there may be rapid cycling between types or a collapse into the most primitive response (usually Freeze, as the last-ditch survival strategy).

Understanding this helps you make sense of the shifts. When your partner suddenly behaves differently than usual, ask: What's their stress level? What just happened that might have made their primary strategy feel unsafe?

9.4 Context Dependent Responses

Some partners have responses that are context-specific.

They may Fight at work but Fawn at home. Or Freeze with authority figures but Fight with equals. Or Flight in their professional life but Freeze in intimate relationships.

This isn't inconsistency; it's adaptation. Different contexts trigger different survival strategies based on what the original trauma taught. Your partner may have learned that fighting back at home was dangerous but effective at school. Or that pleasing was required with one parent but not the other.

If your partner seems like a different person in different contexts, this is likely what's happening. The self they show you may be the one that emerged specifically in response to intimate relationships.

9.5 Recognizing Your Partner's Patterns

Rather than trying to force your partner into a single category, observe their patterns:

What's their default when life is going reasonably well? This is probably their primary type.

What emerges when they're stressed? This may be an amplification of the primary or a shift to secondary.

What happens when they're severely triggered or when the primary response fails? This often reveals the backup strategy.

Are there specific situations that consistently bring out certain responses? Note these and the contexts that trigger them.

Honora created what she called a "mood map" for her partner Remigius: "Fight comes out when he feels criticized. Flight when he's avoiding hard conversations. Freeze when things get really intense. I learned to recognize the shifts and adjust my approach. With Fight Remigius, I stay calm and don't escalate. With Flight Remigius, I try to join him in activity. With Freeze Remigius, I give space and wait."

9.6 When Patterns Shift In Healing

As your partner heals, their 4F patterns will shift.

Healing doesn't mean eliminating these responses. They're natural survival strategies that everyone has. Healing means developing flexibility, the ability to choose the right response for the actual situation rather than defaulting to the same pattern regardless of context.

A healed Fight type can still be assertive when appropriate but can also be vulnerable. A healed Flight type can still be productive but can also rest. A healed Freeze type can still take quiet time but can also engage. A healed Fawn type can still be caring but can also have boundaries.

What you'll see as your partner heals is less intensity, less automaticity, and more choice. The responses still arise, but they're less hijacking and more informing. Your partner becomes able to notice "I'm feeling the urge to fight" and decide whether fighting is actually what's called for.

This is gradual. Don't expect linear progress. There will be periods of great flexibility followed by regression under stress. That's normal.

9.7 Your Own Patterns

Before we leave this topic, a word about your own 4F patterns.

Everyone has these responses. They're part of being human. And your patterns interact with your partner's patterns in ways that can either help or escalate problems.

If you're a Fight type partnered with a Fight type, conflicts may escalate rapidly.

If you're a Fawn type partnered with a Fight type, you may enable their dominance by accommodating.

If you're a Flight type partnered with a Freeze type, you may both escape into your respective avoidances and never connect.

If you're a Freeze type partnered with a Fawn type, neither of you may be assertive enough to address problems.

Understanding your own patterns, and ideally doing your own work on them, makes you a better partner. You can catch yourself when you're defaulting to survival mode rather than presence. You can interrupt escalation cycles. You can model what flexibility looks like.

9.8 Self Assessment Tool

Take a moment to reflect on both your partner's patterns and your own.

For your partner: What response shows up most often in daily life? What emerges under stress? What shows up in intimate moments?

What shows up during conflict? Have you noticed shifts over time or in different contexts?

For yourself: What response shows up most often in daily life? What emerges under stress? What shows up in intimate moments? What shows up during conflict? How do your patterns interact with your partner's patterns?

This reflection isn't about diagnosis. It's about awareness. The more clearly you can see the patterns, the more choice you have in how you respond.

9.9 Key Points

Complexity is normal. Don't try to fit your partner into one box. Most people have hybrid patterns.

Different situations trigger different survival responses. Context, stress level, and specific triggers all affect which response emerges.

Healing means having choice, not eliminating responses. The goal is flexibility, not perfection. Your partner will always have these patterns; they'll just become less automatic.

Chapter 10.0 The Inner Critic Revealed

Leocadia couldn't understand why compliments made her partner Gawain uncomfortable. "You're so talented," she'd say, and he'd wince. "I love how you handled that situation," and he'd find a reason it wasn't good enough. It was like he had a filter that rejected anything positive and amplified anything negative. One night, after years together, Gawain finally explained. "There's a voice in my head that never stops telling me I'm worthless. When you say something nice, the voice gets louder, insisting you're lying or stupid for not seeing the truth. It's exhausting fighting it all day. Sometimes I don't have energy left to fight for your compliments too."

10.1 The Voice From The Past

Every person with C-PTSD carries an inner critic. This isn't the mild self-doubt that everyone experiences. It's a relentless, vicious internal voice that attacks the person constantly, undermining their sense of worth and right to exist.

The inner critic is not native to the person. It's an internalization of the critical, abusive, or neglectful messages from childhood. When a child is constantly told they're stupid, worthless, a burden, or a failure, they eventually absorb these messages. The external abuser becomes an internal presence that continues the abuse long after the person escapes the original environment (Walker, 2013).

Your partner may not even be fully aware of this voice because it's been there so long it seems like objective reality. They may not think "My inner critic is telling me I'm worthless." They may just think "I am worthless." The critic has colonized their self-perception so thoroughly that its voice sounds like truth.

10.2 How Abusers Become Internalized

The process by which external criticism becomes internal is both tragic and logical.

Children are biologically dependent on their caregivers. They cannot survive without them. This creates a powerful drive to maintain the relationship, even when the caregiver is harmful.

When a child is mistreated, they have two options for making sense of their experience. Option one: the caregiver is wrong, bad, or dangerous. Option two: I am wrong, bad, or deserving of this treatment.

Option one is too threatening. It means the person the child depends on for survival is unsafe. The child's psyche can't tolerate this.

Option two, though painful, preserves the fantasy that the caregiver is good and that if only the child could be better, they would receive love. It maintains hope.

So the child concludes: "I'm the problem." And they internalize the caregiver's critical voice as their own, believing it contains truth about who they are (Herman, 1992).

10.3 Forms Of Inner Critic Attack

Pete Walker identifies numerous ways the inner critic attacks. Here are some of the most common:

Perfectionism demands impossibly high standards. Nothing is ever good enough. Any flaw is catastrophic. The person feels they must be perfect to be acceptable.

Catastrophizing anticipates the worst in every situation. Small problems become disasters. Everything will go wrong. Hope is dangerous because disappointment is inevitable.

Harsh self-judgment applies the strictest standards to self while being lenient with others. The person holds themselves to impossible expectations and condemns themselves for any failure.

Self-blame takes responsibility for things that aren't their fault. If something goes wrong, it must be their fault somehow.

Comparison always finds others superior. Everyone else has it together. Everyone else is more competent, more likable, more worthy.

Time urgency creates constant pressure. There's never enough time. The person is always behind, always failing to do enough.

All-or-nothing thinking eliminates middle ground. One mistake means total failure. Partial success is failure. Anything less than perfect is worthless.

Negative mind-reading assumes others are judging negatively. "They must think I'm an idiot." "Everyone noticed my mistake." "You probably regret being with me."

10.4 How The Critic Affects Your Relationship

The inner critic doesn't just attack your partner internally. It bleeds into the relationship in several ways:

"I don't deserve you." Your partner may constantly express disbelief that you're with them, waiting for you to realize your mistake and leave.

Rejection of compliments and love. When you offer praise or affection, it contradicts the critic's narrative. The cognitive dissonance is so uncomfortable that your partner may dismiss or argue with your positive feedback.

Self-sabotage when things are going well. If the relationship is good, the critic predicts disaster. Better to end it preemptively than wait for the inevitable abandonment.

Inability to celebrate achievements. Any success is immediately minimized or attributed to luck, other people, or temporary factors that will soon reverse.

Projecting the critic onto you. Your partner may assume you think all the terrible things the critic says. "You probably think I'm an idiot." They hear criticism even when you haven't given any.

Excessive apologizing. The critic demands contrition for existing. Your partner apologizes constantly, for everything, often for things that require no apology.

10.5 Why Reassurance Does Not Stick

Partners often try to combat the inner critic with reassurance. "You're not stupid, you're brilliant." "I love you." "You're more than good enough."

This feels like the obvious response. The critic says terrible things, so you counter with positive things. Simple.

Except it doesn't work. Or rather, it doesn't stick. Your partner may feel momentarily better, then return to the same negative beliefs. You find yourself saying the same reassuring things over and over, feeling like you're pouring water into a bucket with no bottom.

Here's what's happening: The inner critic has been present for far longer than you have. Its voice carries the weight of childhood authority. It "knows" the "truth" about your partner in a way that feels fundamental.

Your voice, however loving, is a newcomer. The critic dismisses it as naive (you don't really know them), temporary (you'll realize the truth eventually), or proof of your own failings (you must be stupid to believe good things about them).

This isn't about the quality of your reassurance. It's about the architecture of trauma. External positive feedback cannot easily overwrite internally held beliefs that were installed during development.

10.6 The Critic's Misguided Protection

Here's something that may be surprising: the inner critic, however destructive, is attempting to protect your partner.

Remember, the critic was internalized because it helped the child survive. By criticizing themselves first, the child hoped to improve and avoid punishment. By expecting the worst, they avoided the pain of disappointed hope. By holding impossible standards, they maintained an illusion of control: if only they could be perfect, they would finally be safe.

The critic genuinely believes it's helping. It's trying to prevent pain by anticipating it, to motivate improvement through harsh critique, to keep expectations low so disappointment is minimized.

This misguided protection explains why the critic is so persistent. Parts of your partner's psyche believe they need it to survive. Until they develop other ways of feeling safe, the critic will fight to maintain its role.

10.7 What You Might Be Feeling

If your partner has a severe inner critic, you may be experiencing:

Frustration at their constant self-attack. It's painful to watch someone you love treat themselves so badly.

Helplessness when reassurance doesn't help. You try everything and nothing seems to work.

Exhaustion from repeating the same affirmations. How many times can you say "You're good enough" before you run out of energy?

Hurt when they can't receive your love. It can feel like rejection even though it's not about you.

Confusion about why they believe such obviously untrue things. From outside, the critic's claims seem ridiculous. From inside, they feel like truth.

10.8 Supporting Strategies

You can't defeat your partner's inner critic for them. But you can support their battle against it.

Witness without trying to fix. Sometimes your partner just needs someone to know how hard this is. "I hear that the critic is really loud today" validates their experience without trying to argue them out of it.

Offer gentle reality-checking. Not aggressive debate, but soft alternatives. "The critic says you're worthless. I see someone who showed up, tried hard, and did their best."

Be patient with repetition. They may need to hear the same reassurance many times. Each repetition is a small deposit that accumulates over time.

Model self-compassion. Treat yourself the way you want them to treat themselves. Acknowledge your own mistakes kindly, speak positively about yourself, demonstrate that imperfection is okay.

Celebrate small wins. When they manage to counter the critic, even briefly, notice it. "I heard you just accept that compliment without arguing. That's great."

Don't take it personally. When they can't receive your love, it's not about you. The critic is the problem, not your quality as a partner.

Encourage professional support. Inner critic work is often central to C-PTSD therapy. Your partner needs professional help to truly address this.

10.9 Key Principles

The inner critic is not your partner. It's an internalized abuser. What sounds like your partner's voice is actually an echo of people who hurt them long ago.

You can't argue someone out of toxic shame. Logic and reassurance help, but they don't solve the fundamental wound. That requires deeper healing work.

Consistent safety slowly quiets the critic. Your steady, loving presence over time contributes to the sense of safety that allows your partner to question the critic's voice.

Chapter 11.0 Toxic Shame Explored

For years, Theodora thought her partner Cyril was simply private. He didn't talk much about himself, avoided certain topics, and deflected personal questions with jokes or subject changes. It took a health crisis, and the vulnerability that came with it, for the truth to emerge. "I can't let you see me like this," Cyril said, tears streaming. "Once you really see me, you'll be disgusted. Everyone leaves when they see what's underneath." Theodora looked at him: a good man, flawed and human like everyone, wrestling with illness. What was there to be disgusted by? But Cyril wasn't seeing himself through her eyes. He was seeing himself through the eyes of parents who had made him feel, every day, that his very existence was a disappointment.

11.1 Guilt Versus Shame

To understand toxic shame, we first need to distinguish it from guilt.

Guilt says: "I did something bad." It's about behavior. It can be addressed through apology, amends, and changed behavior. Healthy guilt is actually useful because it helps us align our actions with our values.

Shame says: "I am bad." It's about identity. There's nothing to fix because the self itself is the problem. The person feels defective at their core, not for what they did, but for who they are (Brown, 2012).

Everyone experiences some shame. It's a social emotion that helps us regulate behavior within communities. But toxic shame goes far beyond normal social feedback. It's a chronic, pervasive sense of fundamental defectiveness that colors everything.

People with C-PTSD often carry toxic shame as their baseline state. They don't have shame; they are shame.

11.2 How Toxic Shame Develops

Children develop toxic shame when they're treated as though their fundamental nature is wrong.

Neglect teaches shame. The neglected child concludes: "I don't exist because I don't matter. There's something so wrong with me that I don't deserve attention, care, or love."

Abuse teaches shame. The abused child concludes: "I'm being hurt because I deserve to be hurt. There's something bad in me that causes this."

Chronic criticism teaches shame. The criticized child concludes: "Everything about me is wrong. I can never get anything right because I am fundamentally defective."

Emotional invalidation teaches shame. The child whose feelings are dismissed, mocked, or punished concludes: "My inner experience is wrong. There's something broken about how I feel things."

Parentification teaches shame. The child who must parent their own parent concludes: "My needs are burdensome. I should have no needs."

In all these cases, the shame attaches not to specific behaviors but to the self. The child doesn't just feel bad about what happened; they feel that they are bad.

11.3 The Shame Spiral

Toxic shame creates a vicious cycle called the shame spiral.

Something triggers shame (criticism, failure, vulnerability, even positive attention). The person feels overwhelmed by the sense of being defective. To cope with this unbearable feeling, they use defensive strategies: withdrawal, anger, dissociation, self-attack, or compulsive behaviors.

These strategies provide temporary relief but often create more shame. The person who withdrew is now ashamed of their avoidance. The person who lashed out is ashamed of their anger. The person who numbed with substances is ashamed of their coping mechanism.

This additional shame triggers more defensive strategies, which create more shame, in an exhausting downward spiral.

Your partner may be caught in shame spirals frequently. What looks like mood instability or confusing behavior may be the cycling through shame and defense against shame.

11.4 Why Love Can Trigger Shame

One of the cruelest aspects of toxic shame is how it's triggered by love.

When you express love to a shame-bound person, you're offering something that contradicts their deepest belief about themselves. They "know" they're unlovable. Your love doesn't compute.

The cognitive dissonance is intolerable. Something has to give. Either they're wrong about being unlovable (threatening their entire self-concept) or you're wrong about loving them (easier to believe).

So love becomes a trigger. Compliments trigger shame. Gifts trigger shame. Expressions of desire trigger shame. The very things that should feel good instead activate the wound.

Your partner may push you away when you get too close. They may become anxious, irritable, or dissociated during moments of intimacy. They may start fights after particularly connected times. They may sabotage good things because good things don't fit their internal narrative.

Faustina described this experience: "When things are going well in my relationship, I feel the most anxious. Part of me is waiting for the other shoe to drop. Part of me is sure I'm deceiving Erasmus somehow, that he'll eventually see the truth and leave. Being loved is actually harder than being alone, because alone at least matches what I expect."

11.5 Shame Based Behaviors

Toxic shame drives a range of behaviors that can be confusing in relationships:

Hiding parts of self. Your partner may keep significant aspects of themselves secret, not because they're ashamed of specific things they've done, but because they're ashamed of who they are.

Lying even when unnecessary. Shame can make the truth feel dangerous. Your partner may lie about small things, not to deceive you maliciously, but because truth-telling feels vulnerable.

Avoiding vulnerability. Intimacy requires showing one's authentic self. Shame says the authentic self is disgusting. Therefore, intimacy must be avoided.

Rejecting help or gifts. Accepting help means admitting need, which triggers shame. Accepting gifts means accepting that someone values you, which contradicts the shame narrative.

Sexual difficulties. Sex requires vulnerability and being seen in one's body. For the shame-bound person, this can be profoundly threatening.

Sabotaging good things. When life goes well, shame predicts disaster or doesn't trust the goodness. Better to destroy it oneself than wait for inevitable loss.

Perfectionism and over-achievement. Some people try to compensate for their perceived defectiveness by being perfect. If they can just achieve enough, maybe they'll become acceptable.

11.6 The Shame Paradox

Here's the deepest tragedy of toxic shame: it creates a paradox that traps the person.

Shame demands hiding. The person feels too defective to be seen. They must conceal their true self or face rejection.

But healing requires being seen. The wound was created in relationship (being treated as defective). It can only heal in relationship (being accepted as worthy). To heal, the person must show themselves to a safe other and receive acceptance.

This creates an impossible situation. The very thing that would heal the shame (being seen and accepted) is the thing shame makes impossible (because being seen feels too dangerous).

Your partner is caught in this paradox. They want to let you in. They may desperately want to be truly known and accepted. But the shame says: if you really knew me, you'd leave. So they hide. And hiding keeps them sick.

11.7 What You Might Be Feeling

If your partner carries toxic shame, you may be experiencing:

Rejection when they push you away at moments of closeness. It feels like your love is being refused.

Confusion about what they're hiding. You sense there are walls, but you can't understand what's behind them.

Hurt by the lies or secrets, even when they're small. The pattern of hiding feels like distrust.

Helplessness when your love isn't enough. You're offering exactly what they need, and they can't take it in.

Grief for the intimacy that feels blocked. You want more depth but can't seem to get past their defenses.

11.8 Shame Healing Practices

Shame heals through safe exposure. The person needs to be seen, in their vulnerability and perceived defectiveness, and not rejected.

This is slow, delicate work, primarily done in therapy. But you can contribute:

Create safety for vulnerability. Respond to whatever they share with acceptance rather than shock, judgment, or advice. Even if they tell you difficult things, stay regulated and present.

Not reacting to confessions. When they do let you see something they're ashamed of, don't make a big deal of it in either direction. Neither dismissing ("That's nothing") nor dramatizing ("Oh my God"). Just receive it and continue loving them.

Celebrate vulnerability. When they take a risk and show you something real, acknowledge it: "Thank you for telling me that. I know that was hard."

Understand relapses into hiding. They will retreat. The shame will push them back behind walls. This isn't failure; it's the nature of the healing process.

Model accepting your own imperfections. Let them see you make mistakes and treat yourself with kindness. Show them that flawed humans are still lovable.

11.9 Key Principles

Shame tells your partner they are unlovable at their core. This isn't a thought they're having; it's a fundamental belief about their identity.

95

Your consistent acceptance is medicine. You cannot cure the shame, but every time you accept them despite their "defects," you provide evidence that challenges the shame narrative.

Healing shame takes years, not months. This is deep work. Progress will be slow and nonlinear. Patience is essential.

Chapter 12.0 Attachment Wounds in Relationships

The first six months with Julius were perfect. Apollonia had never felt so seen, so cherished, so connected. Then something shifted. As the relationship deepened, Julius became increasingly anxious. He needed constant reassurance. He questioned whether she really loved him. He panicked if she didn't text back quickly. And yet, whenever she moved toward him to offer the closeness he seemed to crave, he pulled away. "I need space," he'd say, after days of seeking reassurance. It was like loving someone with contradictory programming. She'd later learn that's exactly what it was. Julius's childhood had taught him that people who loved him would hurt him. He desperately wanted connection and was terrified of it in equal measure.

12.1 Attachment Theory Basics

To understand your partner's relationship patterns, you need to understand attachment theory.

Attachment theory was developed by John Bowlby in the mid-twentieth century and expanded by Mary Ainsworth's research. The core insight is that humans are wired for connection from birth. We need close bonds with caregivers to survive and develop. The quality of these early bonds shapes how we approach relationships throughout life (Bowlby, 1969).

Based on how their caregivers responded to their needs, children develop attachment styles that become templates for all future relationships. These aren't conscious beliefs; they're implicit expectations encoded in the nervous system.

Secure attachment develops when caregivers are consistently responsive. The child learns that they can express needs and have them met, that relationships are safe, and that they are worthy of love. As adults, securely attached people generally trust their partners, communicate openly, and handle conflict constructively.

Insecure attachment develops when caregivers are inconsistent, unavailable, or frightening. The child develops strategies to manage the anxiety of uncertain connection. These strategies persist into adulthood as attachment styles that can complicate relationships.

12.2 Insecure Attachment Styles

Three main insecure attachment styles are identified in the research:

Anxious attachment (sometimes called preoccupied) develops when caregivers are inconsistent. Sometimes present and loving, sometimes absent or unavailable. The child learns that relationships are unreliable and must be constantly monitored. As adults, anxiously attached people tend to crave closeness intensely, seek frequent reassurance, fear abandonment, and become distressed when partners aren't immediately available. They may appear "needy" or "clingy" (Hazan & Shaver, 1987).

Avoidant attachment (sometimes called dismissive) develops when caregivers are emotionally unavailable or rejecting of needs. The child learns to suppress their attachment needs and become self-sufficient. As adults, avoidantly attached people tend to value independence, feel uncomfortable with too much closeness, withdraw when partners seek intimacy, and minimize the importance of relationships. They may appear "cold" or "distant."

Disorganized attachment (sometimes called fearful-avoidant) develops when caregivers are frightening or themselves frightened. The child faces an impossible situation: the person they need to go to for safety is also the source of fear. There's no coherent strategy. As adults, disorganized attachment creates a chaotic pattern where the person desperately wants closeness but is terrified of it. They may oscillate between anxious and avoidant behaviors, sometimes within the same conversation (Main & Hesse, 1990).

12.3 C-PTSD And Disorganized Attachment

Disorganized attachment is the signature attachment pattern of Complex PTSD.

When a child is abused or severely neglected by caregivers, they're caught in the impossible bind described above. They need attachment to survive but attaching is dangerous. Their nervous system never organizes a coherent strategy for relationships.

The result in adulthood is the push-pull dynamic that partners of C-PTSD survivors know so well. Your partner:

Desperately wants closeness AND is terrified of it. Seeks reassurance AND doesn't believe it. Clings to you AND pushes you away. Fears abandonment AND creates distance. Wants to trust you AND can't trust anyone.

This isn't inconsistency or manipulation. It's the manifestation of two powerful, contradictory drives running simultaneously. They want love and they fear it, and both are completely real at the same time.

12.4 The Come Here Go Away Dance

Living with a disorganized attachment partner means participating in what some therapists call the "come here, go away" dance.

The sequence often goes like this: Your partner seeks closeness. You respond warmly. As intimacy increases, their attachment fear activates. They pull away or push you away. You feel rejected and step back. Their abandonment fear activates. They seek closeness again. And the cycle continues.

Galatea described this pattern: "It was like Faramond had two modes: desperately needing me and desperately needing distance from me. I never knew which I'd get. He'd spend days wanting constant connection, then suddenly announce he needed space and retreat completely. If I gave him the space, he'd eventually panic and come seeking me again. It was exhausting and confusing until I understood it wasn't about me at all."

The important thing to recognize is that this pattern isn't a choice. Your partner isn't playing games. Their nervous system is caught between two survival strategies that can't be reconciled without healing work.

12.5 How Attachment Plays Out Over Time

Attachment patterns tend to be most visible at certain relationship stages:

Beginning of relationship. Many couples report a "honeymoon period" where the disorganized partner seems fine. This is because attachment behaviors are activated by emotional investment. Before the relationship feels important, the attachment system is relatively quiet.

Deepening commitment. As the relationship becomes more significant, the attachment system wakes up. This is often when problems emerge. Moving in together, saying "I love you," meeting families, and other commitment markers can trigger intense attachment anxiety.

Major milestones. Engagement, marriage, buying a home, having children, these represent deepening entanglement and therefore greater attachment activation. Partners often report crises around these transitions.

Conflict and repair. How couples handle disagreements is heavily influenced by attachment. Anxious partners may escalate seeking reassurance. Avoidant partners may withdraw. Disorganized partners may do both rapidly.

Threat to relationship. Any perceived threat to the relationship (job stress, illness, outside attraction, conflict) will activate attachment strategies at full force.

12.6 Earned Secure Attachment

Here's the hopeful news: attachment patterns can change.

Researchers have identified what they call "earned secure attachment." These are people who had difficult childhoods but, through therapy, healthy relationships, and personal growth, have developed secure attachment patterns as adults. Their history was insecure, but their current functioning is secure (Roisman et al., 2002).

This means your partner isn't doomed to disorganized attachment forever. With proper treatment, consistent relationship safety, and time, they can develop more secure ways of relating.

The therapy work involves understanding their attachment history, developing awareness of their patterns, and building new relational experiences that contradict the old programming. This is usually attachment-focused therapy, often including EMDR, IFS, or other approaches that address developmental trauma.

Your relationship contributes to this healing. Every time you're consistently safe, every time you repair after rupture, every time you stay present when they push away, you're providing evidence that relationships can be different. This evidence gradually updates their attachment system.

12.7 Your Own Attachment Pattern

Your attachment style also affects the relationship.

Take a moment to consider your own patterns:

Do you tend toward anxious attachment (seeking reassurance, fearing abandonment, sensitive to signs of rejection)?

Do you tend toward avoidant attachment (valuing independence, uncomfortable with too much closeness, withdrawing when things get intense)?

Or are you relatively secure (comfortable with intimacy and independence, able to communicate needs, generally trusting)?

The dance you do with your partner is influenced by both of your styles.

If you're secure and your partner is disorganized, your stability can provide an anchor for their chaos.

If you're anxious and your partner is disorganized, you may both spiral into abandonment fears, creating escalating distress.

If you're avoidant and your partner is disorganized, your withdrawals may trigger their abandonment fears while their neediness triggers your need for space.

Understanding both patterns helps you see the dance you're in and make conscious choices about steps.

12.8 Attachment Patterns Assessment

Consider these questions for yourself:

When stressed in relationships, do you typically seek more closeness or more distance?

How comfortable are you depending on others? Do others seem to want more closeness than you?

How would you describe your parents' availability and responsiveness when you were a child?

What were your previous relationship patterns?

And for your partner:

When stressed in relationships, do they typically seek more closeness, more distance, or both confusingly?

How do they respond when you move closer? When you move away?

What do you know about their childhood attachment experiences?

What patterns have you observed over your time together?

12.9 Key Principles

Your partner's push-pull isn't about you. It's about attachment terror. They're not trying to confuse you; they're caught between two powerful, conflicting drives.

Safety must be proven slowly over time. One positive experience doesn't update an attachment system built over years of development. This requires patience.

Both of you have attachment patterns affecting the relationship. Understanding both your styles helps you navigate the dance more consciously.

Chapter 13.0 Trauma Informed Communication

Berenice thought she was a good communicator. She'd read the relationship books, practiced "I" statements, learned reflective listening. But none of it seemed to work with her partner Marius. The techniques that were supposed to de-escalate conflict seemed to make things worse. The conversations that should have brought them closer left them further apart. It wasn't until she learned about trauma-informed communication that things began to shift. The regular rules, she discovered, don't always apply when trauma is in the room.

13.1 Why Regular Rules Often Fail

Most communication advice assumes both partners have nervous systems that are relatively regulated and online.

The advice says: use "I" statements, listen reflectively, stay calm, talk about your feelings. These are good principles. They work well for couples navigating normal relationship challenges.

But C-PTSD creates conditions where these principles break down:

Your partner's prefrontal cortex may be offline during activation. The part of the brain that processes language and logic isn't fully functional when the survival brain has taken over.

Reflective listening can feel patronizing when someone is dysregulated. "I hear that you're angry" may be met with "Don't patronize me!"

"I" statements can still trigger shame. "I feel hurt when you..." can still sound like "You hurt me," which triggers defensive reactions.

Requesting emotional vulnerability during activation is counterproductive. "Tell me how you're really feeling" when someone is in fight mode just intensifies the fight.

Trauma-informed communication requires adapting these principles to the reality of how trauma affects the brain and nervous system.

13.2 Core Principles

Several principles guide trauma-informed communication:

Safety first, always. Physical and emotional safety must be established before any content can be addressed. If your partner doesn't feel safe, they can't hear you.

Regulation before reason. When someone is activated, their reasoning capacity is diminished. Helping them regulate (calm their nervous system) must come before trying to discuss issues.

Curiosity over judgment. Approaching your partner with genuine curiosity about their experience, rather than judgment about their behavior, creates safety for opening up.

Repair over perfection. You will make mistakes. Ruptures will happen. What matters is not avoiding all ruptures but repairing them when they occur.

Timing matters as much as content. The best-worded message delivered at the wrong time will fail. The most important skill may be knowing when to talk and when to wait.

13.3 Communication In Different States

Your communication approach should vary depending on your partner's state:

When your partner is regulated (calm, present, connected): This is when productive conversation is possible. You can discuss difficult topics, process past conflicts, and have deeper conversations. Take advantage of these windows.

During mild activation (slightly stressed, a bit reactive, but still functional): Be careful. Stick to essentials. Check in about timing. Keep it short. Watch for signs of escalation.

During full flashback or activation (clearly triggered, not present, survival mode engaged): Stop all content-focused communication. This is not the time to resolve issues. Focus only on helping them regulate and feel safe. We'll discuss specific approaches below.

After a rupture (following a conflict or activated exchange): Give space for regulation first. Then move toward repair. Don't pretend it didn't happen, but don't immediately process either. Reconnect, then talk.

13.4 Techniques That Help

Several specific techniques support trauma-informed communication:

Reflective listening without fixing. "It sounds like you felt unseen when that happened." Full stop. Don't add "but" or "actually" or "let me explain." Just reflect and let it land.

Modified "I" statements. Instead of "I feel hurt when you yell," try "When voices get loud, I notice I start to feel disconnected from you." This focuses on the experience without making your partner the subject of complaint.

Time-outs that aren't abandonment. "I need to pause this conversation. I'm still here, I'm not going anywhere, and I want to come back to this when we can both think more clearly. Can we take twenty minutes?"

Asking permission before difficult topics. "I'd like to talk about what happened yesterday. Is now an okay time?" Giving your partner agency in the timing creates safety.

Soft starts. Research by John Gottman shows that conversations tend to end the way they begin (Gottman, 1999). Start gently: "I've been thinking about something I'd like to share with you" rather than "We need to talk about this problem."

Slowing down. Trauma survivors often have heightened responsiveness to pace. Slow your speech, pause between thoughts, leave space for processing.

13.5 What Not To Say

Certain phrases tend to backfire with C-PTSD partners:

"Calm down." This is dismissive and rarely calms anyone. It implies they're choosing to be upset.

"You're overreacting." Maybe they are, from an objective standpoint. Saying so doesn't help and increases shame.

"Just let it go." They would if they could. Emotional flashbacks don't release on command.

"But I'm not like them." Even if true, your partner's nervous system can't process this during activation. It may even feel like you're dismissing their experience.

"That was years ago." Trauma doesn't care about chronology. The body keeps the score regardless of how much time has passed.

"You always" or "You never." Absolutes trigger defensiveness and rarely reflect reality.

"I'm sorry you feel that way." This is not an apology. It's a dismissal that sounds like an apology.

"What's wrong with you?" This confirms the core shame belief that something is fundamentally wrong with them.

13.6 During Active Flashback

When your partner is in full emotional flashback, communication shifts dramatically:

Stop all content. Don't try to resolve whatever triggered the flashback. Don't explain yourself. Don't discuss the issue. Content is inaccessible right now.

Speak softly and simply. Short sentences. Calm tone. Basic words. "I'm here. You're safe. This will pass."

Avoid excessive eye contact if it increases activation. Some trauma survivors find direct eye contact threatening when triggered.

Offer grounding options without forcing. "Want to squeeze my hand?" "Can you feel your feet?" If they don't respond or refuse, don't push.

Regulate your own nervous system. Your calm is contagious. Your escalation will escalate them. Focus on keeping yourself grounded.

Be patient. Flashbacks run their course. Sometimes all you can do is weather it together.

Don't expect them to remember the conversation. Flashback amnesia is real. They may not recall what you said or what happened.

13.7 Repair After Ruptures

Ruptures (moments of disconnection, conflict, or hurt) are inevitable. How you repair them determines relationship health.

Wait for regulation. Don't attempt repair while either of you is still activated.

Acknowledge what happened. "That was hard. We both got pretty escalated."

Take responsibility for your part without making it about blame. "I know my voice got loud, and that didn't help."

Invite their experience. "What was that like for you?" Then listen.

Validate without necessarily agreeing. "I understand why you felt unsafe, even though I wasn't intending that."

Reconnect before resolving. Sometimes repair is just reconnection: a hug, a shared moment, assurance of love. Resolution of the actual issue may need to wait for another time.

Learn for next time. "What might help if this comes up again?" Planning together builds teamwork.

13.8 Conversation Templates

Here are some templates for common situations:

Raising a difficult topic: "There's something on my mind that I'd like to share. It's a bit hard to talk about, and I want to do it carefully. Is now okay, or would another time work better?"

When they seem triggered: "I notice something shifted. Are you okay? Do you need anything from me right now?"

Taking a break: "I'm starting to feel really activated, and I want to pause so I don't say something hurtful. I'm not leaving, and I do want to talk. Can we come back to this in [specific time]?"

After a rupture: "Last night was hard. I'm still committed to us, and I want to understand your experience. Can we talk about what happened?"

When they can't receive your love: "I notice when I tell you I love you, something happens in you. Can you tell me about that? I'm curious, not criticizing."

13.9 Key Principles

Your partner may not be able to hear you during activation. The brain under threat processes information differently. Timing matters.

Timing matters as much as content. A perfectly worded message at the wrong time will fail. Wait for windows of regulation.

Repair is more important than prevention. You can't prevent all ruptures. You can repair them and, over time, strengthen the relationship through successful repairs.

Chapter 14.0 Intimacy and Physical Connection

For the first year, Honora assumed the physical difficulties were about attraction. Maybe Osric wasn't as into her as she'd hoped. Maybe she was doing something wrong. The way he'd freeze during intimate moments, the times she'd notice him checking out mid-act, the pattern of avoidance followed by guilt followed by avoidance. Then, on a night she gently asked what was happening for him, Osric began to sob. "I want to be close to you. But sometimes my body just... leaves. I'm there, but I'm not there. And then I feel so broken." It wasn't about attraction. It was about trauma living in the body.

14.1 Why Intimacy Is Complicated

Physical intimacy is often challenging for C-PTSD survivors, and this is true whether or not they experienced sexual trauma specifically.

Intimacy requires vulnerability. It requires letting someone see your body, hear your sounds, witness your pleasure, know your desires. For someone whose core belief is that they are defective and unworthy, this exposure can feel terrifying.

Intimacy involves the body. Trauma lives in the body. Sensations, positions, touches, or states of arousal can trigger body memories that pull a person out of the present moment.

Intimacy involves another person in very close proximity. For someone whose trauma was relational, having another person that close, however loving, can activate threat responses.

Intimacy involves losing control. Pleasure, arousal, and orgasm all involve a degree of surrender. For someone who survived by maintaining vigilance and control, surrender feels dangerous.

Understanding these dynamics helps reframe intimacy challenges. It's not that your partner doesn't find you attractive. It's not that they don't want closeness. It's that their nervous system has associations with intimacy that make it complicated.

14.2 Common Challenges

Several patterns commonly appear in the intimacy lives of C-PTSD survivors:

Dissociation during sex. Your partner may "leave" during intimate moments, going blank, becoming distant, or seeming like they're not present. They may report feeling like they're watching from outside their body.

Avoidance of physical touch. Your partner may limit or avoid physical affection, from sex to cuddling to casual touch. The body-to-body contact feels threatening.

Using sex to manage emotions. Conversely, some survivors use sexual activity as a coping mechanism, soothing anxiety or numbing pain through physical stimulation. This can look like high interest but may not actually be connected intimacy.

Body shame and disconnection. Your partner may struggle to be comfortable in their body, feeling disconnected from physical sensations or ashamed of how they look.

Flashbacks triggered by physical sensations. Certain touches, positions, or sensations may trigger emotional flashbacks, pulling your partner into past experiences of trauma.

Difficulty being present. Even without full dissociation, your partner may struggle to stay in the moment, their mind racing or distracted.

Arousal difficulties. Trauma can affect the body's ability to become aroused or to relax enough for arousal to feel pleasurable.

14.3 Understanding Without Personalizing

The most important thing you can do around intimacy challenges is understand that they're not about you.

When your partner freezes during sex, it's not because you're doing something wrong. When they avoid touch, it's not because they don't find you attractive. When they can't be present, it's not because they're bored or disconnected from you.

These are trauma responses playing out in the body. The same survival strategies we've discussed, fight, flight, freeze, fawn, show up during intimacy in specific ways. Freeze is perhaps most common: the body goes still and absent as a way to survive something that feels threatening.

Personalizing these responses creates additional problems. You feel rejected and hurt. You may withdraw or become resentful. Your partner senses your hurt and feels more shame, which makes intimacy even harder. The cycle reinforces itself.

Instead, try to hold the understanding: "My partner's body is responding to old wounds. This isn't about me."

14.4 Creating Safety In Physical Intimacy

Several practices help create safety for intimate connection:

Consent as ongoing conversation. Check in regularly, not just at the beginning. "Is this still okay?" "Do you want to continue?" "What would feel good right now?" Make consent a continuous dialogue rather than a one-time permission.

Pace controlled by the survivor. Let your partner set the pace of physical escalation. Don't rush toward sex. Follow their lead. This gives them control, which is crucial for someone whose trauma involved powerlessness.

Safe words and signals. Agree on a word or signal that means "stop immediately, no questions." This provides an exit hatch that makes it safer to try things.

Check in about dissociation. If you notice your partner drifting, gently name it: "Are you still with me?" This can sometimes help them come back to the present.

Reconnection practices after difficult experiences. If intimacy goes badly, how do you reconnect? Having a plan (maybe just holding each other, maybe taking a break and coming back together) reduces the fallout.

Debriefing afterward. Sometimes talking about what worked and what didn't, when not in the heat of the moment, helps build understanding and improve future experiences.

14.5 Non Sexual Physical Connection

It's worth emphasizing that physical intimacy is broader than sex.

Non-sexual touch, cuddling, hand-holding, massage, sitting close, can be deeply connecting and may actually be easier for your partner than sexual activity.

Building safety with non-sexual touch creates a foundation for sexual intimacy. If your partner can relax into a hug, they're practicing the same nervous system regulation that will help them relax during sex.

Some couples find that taking sex off the table for a period, and focusing only on non-sexual connection, reduces pressure and paradoxically improves their eventual sexual connection.

14.6 When Professional Help Is Needed

Some intimacy challenges require professional support:

If there's a history of sexual trauma specifically, working with a therapist who specializes in this area is important. Sexual trauma creates particular challenges that benefit from targeted treatment.

If dissociation during intimacy is severe, this may indicate a need for trauma processing work before intimacy can feel safe.

If intimacy challenges are causing significant relationship distress, couples therapy with a trauma-informed therapist can help.

If your partner has never talked about the sexual aspects of their trauma, doing so with you (rather than a professional) first may not be advisable. Therapy provides the appropriate container for that processing.

Sex therapy, specifically trauma-informed sex therapy, is a specialty that addresses exactly these challenges. If this is a significant issue for your relationship, it's worth exploring.

14.7 Special Considerations For Sexual Abuse Survivors

If your partner experienced sexual abuse, the challenges may be particularly complex.

Their body may have learned to associate intimate touch with violation. Sensations that should be pleasurable may be contaminated by trauma.

They may have complicated feelings about arousal if their body responded to abuse. This creates deep shame that requires careful therapeutic work.

Triggers may be very specific and unpredictable. Certain words, positions, touches, or even times of day may activate trauma responses.

Trust in the intimate context may be especially difficult since their previous experience of intimate situations involved betrayal.

Recovery is possible, but it takes time and patience. Many sexual abuse survivors develop satisfying intimate lives, but the path there is often longer and requires more professional support.

14.8 Key Principles

Intimacy problems are about trauma, not attraction to you. Your partner's nervous system has learned associations that make physical closeness complicated.

Safety and control are essential ingredients. Consent, pacing, and signals help your partner feel enough safety to be present.

Patience and creativity can rebuild connection over time. Intimacy may never look exactly like what you imagined, but meaningful physical connection is possible.

Chapter 15.0 Parenting Together With C-PTSD

When Jessamine became pregnant, she thought Benedictus's healing would accelerate. Children bring joy, she reasoned. Family would fill the voids in his past. She wasn't prepared for how triggering parenting would be. Their infant's cries sent Benedictus into panic states. Their toddler's defiance activated his rage. Their child's neediness overwhelmed him with feelings he couldn't name. "I can't do this," he told her one night, tears streaming. "I can't give them what I never got." But he could, and he did, with support, with therapy, with patience from both of them. Parenting with C-PTSD is hard. It's also one of the most powerful opportunities for healing.

15.1 Unique Parenting Challenges

Parenting is challenging for everyone. For survivors of childhood trauma, it presents particular difficulties.

Children's normal behaviors can trigger trauma responses. Crying, neediness, tantrums, defiance, these are developmentally appropriate behaviors that may resemble dynamics from the survivor's own childhood. The parent may be triggered into their 4F responses by their own child.

Fear of repeating family patterns looms large. Most C-PTSD survivors desperately want to parent differently than they were parented. This fear can create constant anxiety about "am I doing this right?" and paralyzing self-doubt when mistakes happen.

Overprotection or under-protection may occur. Some survivors become hypervigilant about protecting their children from any harm. Others, having normalized mistreatment, may not recognize when their children need protection.

Discipline is complicated. Many survivors struggle to set appropriate limits without either being too harsh (echoing their own upbringing) or too permissive (overcompensating).

Physical and emotional exhaustion is intensified. Parenting is exhausting for everyone. For someone already managing trauma symptoms, the additional demands can push them past their capacity.

Children's developmental stages may trigger age-specific memories. When a child reaches the age the parent was when trauma occurred, old wounds may surface.

15.2 How Partners Can Support

As the non-traumatized (or less-traumatized) parent, you play a crucial role.

Tag-team parenting during hard moments. When you see your partner becoming activated by your child's behavior, step in. "I've got this one." Give them space to regulate without the immediate demand of the child.

Be the regulated parent when needed. Children need at least one parent who can stay calm during their storms. If your partner can't do that in a given moment, you can.

Don't undermine in front of children. Even if you disagree with how your partner handled something, address it later, privately. United front with children, processing between parents afterward.

Private conversations about parenting differences. You will have different instincts about parenting. Some of your partner's instincts may be trauma-driven. Discuss these gently and privately.

Recognize the emotional labor your partner is doing. Parenting while managing trauma is extraordinarily hard. Acknowledge their effort.

Support their therapy attendance. Parenting triggers may require additional therapeutic work. Make space for that.

15.3 Breaking The Cycle

One of the deepest drives for C-PTSD survivors who become parents is the determination to break the intergenerational cycle of trauma.

This is entirely possible. Many trauma survivors become excellent parents. Research shows that with awareness and support, parents can raise securely attached children even if they themselves were not securely attached (Roisman et al., 2002).

What helps break the cycle:

Awareness of patterns. Your partner knowing their triggers, their tendencies, their family patterns creates the possibility of choosing differently.

Accountability without shame. When your partner slips into old patterns, they need to be able to recognize it without drowning in shame. Your compassionate feedback helps.

Celebrating progress. Breaking generational patterns is heroic work. Notice when your partner responds to your child differently than they were responded to.

Professional support. Parenting as a trauma survivor often benefits from therapeutic support, either ongoing individual therapy or specifically parent-focused work.

15.4 Talking To Children

At some point, children may need some understanding of their parent's struggles.

Age-appropriate language is key. Young children don't need details. "Mommy/Daddy sometimes has big feelings and needs to take a break" is enough.

Emphasize that it's not the child's fault. Children naturally assume they caused parent's distress. Make clear: "This isn't because of anything you did."

Model emotional honesty. "I'm feeling overwhelmed right now and need a few minutes" is healthier than pretending everything is fine while visibly struggling.

Don't burden children with adult problems. Children shouldn't become their parent's emotional support. Keep conversations simple and reassuring.

Answer questions simply and honestly. If a child asks about a parent's behavior or absence, provide simple, truthful answers without oversharing.

15.5 When To Seek Family Therapy

Some situations benefit from family therapy:

When children are showing signs of distress. Anxiety, behavioral problems, or attachment difficulties in children may indicate that the family system needs support.

When conflicts about parenting are causing relationship strain. A family therapist can help you find aligned approaches.

When a child is old enough to be aware of the parent's struggles and has questions. A therapist can help guide these conversations.

When your partner's symptoms are significantly impacting parenting. If the C-PTSD is affecting their ability to parent effectively, family-focused intervention helps.

15.6 Key Principles

Your partner likely desperately wants to be a good parent. The fear and struggle come from caring, not from indifference.

Parenting can be both triggering and healing. Children offer opportunities to both revisit wounds and heal them by doing differently.

Children benefit from one securely attached parent. Your stable presence provides your children with security even when your partner is struggling.

Chapter 16.0 Managing Triggers Daily

Every December, Clotilde dreaded Christmas. Not because she disliked the holiday, but because she knew what it would do to her partner Erasmus. The family gatherings, the forced cheer, the expectations of togetherness sent him spiraling for weeks. One year, she decided enough was enough. Instead of hoping things would be different, they sat down together and made a plan. Which events would they attend? For how long? What signals would Erasmus use when he needed to leave? What would Clotilde say to questioning relatives? That Christmas wasn't perfect. But it was the first one in years that didn't end with Erasmus locked in the bedroom for three days.

16.1 The Rhythm Of Daily Triggers

Living with C-PTSD means living with triggers woven into the fabric of everyday life. These aren't just the obvious reminders of trauma. They're hidden in morning routines, household chores, and ordinary conversations. Understanding the common daily triggers helps you anticipate rather than just react.

Morning routines and transitions can be surprisingly difficult. The shift from sleep to wakefulness is a vulnerable time. Your partner may wake already activated, remnants of nightmares or simply the body's alarm system coming online. Transitions throughout the day (leaving for work, coming home, shifting between activities) require nervous system adjustments that can be taxing.

Household responsibilities carry hidden weight. For someone whose childhood included criticism for every failure, an unwashed dish isn't just a dish. It's evidence of inadequacy. Forgetting to pay a bill, leaving clothes on the floor, running out of milk can trigger shame spirals completely out of proportion to the actual situation.

Social events and family gatherings present concentrated challenges. Multiple people, unpredictable conversations, expectations of performance, and often, contact with family members connected to the original trauma. Even pleasant social situations require energy that trauma survivors may not have.

Work stress doesn't stay at work. Your partner may come home already depleted, their nervous system running hot from eight hours of managing triggers in the workplace. What looks like being fine at the office may be followed by collapse at home.

Financial discussions touch on security and survival. For someone whose childhood involved scarcity, unpredictability, or financial chaos, conversations about money can activate primal fear responses.

Health appointments combine vulnerability, authority figures, loss of control, and bodily exposure. Medical settings can be particularly triggering for those with histories of physical abuse or medical trauma.

16.2 Holidays And Anniversaries

Certain times of year carry particular intensity.

Family-oriented holidays like Thanksgiving, Christmas, Hanukkah, and Mother's Day or Father's Day can be excruciating. These occasions celebrate family connection. For someone whose family was the source of trauma, the cultural pressure to feel grateful and joyful creates painful cognitive dissonance.

Anniversaries of traumatic events may not even be consciously remembered. The body often knows what the mind has forgotten. Your partner may become symptomatic at certain times of year without knowing why. If you notice annual patterns, gently exploring whether something significant happened during that time can bring helpful awareness.

Seasonal changes affect mood and energy. Shorter days in winter can exacerbate depression. The return of spring might trigger body memories of trauma that occurred in that season.

Faustina noticed her partner Marius became increasingly agitated every September. Neither of them understood why until his therapist helped him realize that September was when he'd been sent to live with an abusive relative as a child. His body remembered the season of abandonment even though his conscious mind had buried the connection.

16.3 Creating A Trigger Plan

Rather than reacting to triggers as they arise, proactive planning reduces crisis frequency and severity.

A trigger management plan is a document you create together that identifies known triggers, warning signs, helpful responses, and emergency protocols. This isn't about controlling every variable. It's about having a shared understanding and agreed-upon strategies before activation happens.

Start by mapping known triggers. What situations, people, places, times, or topics reliably cause problems? Be specific. Not just "family" but "when my mother asks about my job." Not just "criticism" but "feedback about housekeeping."

Identify early warning signs. What does your partner look like when they're beginning to get triggered? What physical signs appear? What behavioral changes? The earlier you can recognize activation, the more options you have.

Agree on helpful responses. What does your partner want from you when they're triggered? Some people want closeness. Others need space. Some want to talk. Others need silence. Knowing this in advance prevents mismatched expectations.

Establish emergency protocols. What if nothing works and there's a full crisis? Who do you call? Where can your partner go to feel safe? What are the steps for de-escalation?

Write it down. A plan that exists only in your heads is less useful than one you can reference. Keep it somewhere accessible.

16.4 Environmental Modifications

Your physical environment can either support regulation or undermine it.

Quiet spaces matter. Having a designated place in your home where your partner can retreat when overwhelmed makes a difference. This might be a bedroom, a corner with comfortable seating, or even a closet made cozy. The key is a space that feels safe and removed from stimulation.

Predictable routines provide stability. Trauma survivors often benefit from knowing what to expect. Regular mealtimes, consistent bedtimes, and predictable schedules reduce the ambient anxiety that comes from uncertainty. This doesn't mean rigid inflexibility. It means having a baseline of predictability to return to.

Sensory considerations help. Some people with C-PTSD are sensitive to noise, light, textures, or smells. Paying attention to the sensory environment (soft lighting, reduced clutter, comfortable textures) can lower baseline activation.

Exit strategies from difficult situations should be planned in advance. Before attending a family gathering, know how you'll leave if needed. Have a signal between you ("I'm getting a headache" might mean "I need to go now"). Park in a spot that allows easy departure. Don't rely on others for transportation.

Galatea and her partner Theophilus developed a code phrase for family events: "I think I left the stove on." Whenever Theophilus said this, Galatea knew he was at his limit and would immediately start making their excuses to leave. Having this agreement in place meant Theophilus never had to explain or justify his need to exit.

16.5 Accommodation Versus Avoidance

Here's where things get complicated. Some accommodation of triggers is loving and appropriate. Excessive accommodation becomes avoidance that ultimately harms.

Loving accommodation looks like: adjusting holiday plans to reduce exposure to toxic family members, giving your partner space to regulate after a hard day, not bringing up sensitive topics at vulnerable times, and creating environmental supports that help them function.

Harmful avoidance looks like: never attending any social event because something might be triggering, eliminating all stress from your partner's life so they never build tolerance, making all decisions for them to protect them from any discomfort, and organizing your entire life around preventing any trigger from ever occurring.

The difference lies in the trajectory. Accommodation should support your partner's gradual expansion of capacity. Avoidance keeps them (and you) increasingly constricted.

A helpful question to ask: Is this accommodation helping my partner engage more fully with life over time? Or is it helping them engage less?

Recovery from C-PTSD involves slowly expanding the window of tolerance, the range of experiences a person can handle without becoming dysregulated (Siegel, 2012). This requires some exposure to manageable challenges. If you remove all challenges, the window never expands.

16.6 When Protection Becomes Enabling

There's a fine line between supporting your partner and enabling avoidance that keeps them stuck.

Signs that protection has become enabling include: your partner's world is getting smaller over time rather than larger, you're doing more and more things for them that they could do themselves, they show no motivation to build their own coping capacity, your own life is increasingly constrained by their limitations, and there's an expectation that you will manage all triggers rather than them developing skills.

Enabling often comes from love. You don't want to see your partner suffer, so you remove all potential sources of suffering. But this approach backfires. It confirms their belief that they can't cope. It prevents them from discovering their own strength. And it exhausts you.

The alternative isn't cruel exposure. It's collaborative building of capacity. Your partner should be an active participant in trigger management, not a passive recipient of your protection.

Ask yourself: Am I doing this for my partner, or am I doing this with my partner?

16.7 Practical Trigger Mapping

Use these questions to create your own trigger identification map:

What situations reliably cause distress for your partner? List specific scenarios.

What people are triggering? This might include family members, authority figures, or even people with certain characteristics.

What physical environments are difficult? Crowded spaces, medical offices, childhood locations?

What times of day or year are harder? Mornings, evenings, certain seasons, anniversaries?

What topics of conversation are risky? Money, family, health, the future, the past?

What sensory experiences cause problems? Loud noises, certain smells, physical sensations?

For each trigger identified, note: What does early activation look like? What helps during activation? What makes it worse? What's the recovery time afterward?

This map becomes your guide for anticipating and planning around difficult situations.

16.8 Holiday Survival Strategies

Holidays deserve special attention because they concentrate so many triggers.

Before the holiday: Decide together which events to attend and for how long. Set realistic expectations (aiming for "tolerable" rather than "wonderful"). Prepare responses for intrusive questions. Identify allies who understand. Have an exit plan.

During the holiday: Check in with each other regularly. Watch for early warning signs. Take breaks as needed. Use grounding techniques in the moment. Don't override your partner's signals that they need to leave.

After the holiday: Allow recovery time. Don't immediately process what went wrong. Prioritize rest and regulation. Celebrate what went well.

Consider creating new traditions that don't carry old baggage. Maybe your holiday doesn't include extended family. Maybe you celebrate on a different day. Maybe you redefine what the holiday means for your particular family.

Dorothea and her partner Ivo decided to spend every Thanksgiving at a cabin in the mountains, just the two of them. They let go of the guilt about not attending family events and created their own tradition that actually felt nourishing rather than depleting.

16.9 Emergency Response Planning

For times when triggers overwhelm coping capacity, have a plan ready:

Immediate steps: What helps in the first moments of crisis? Grounding techniques, safe space, specific comfort items?

Communication protocol: How will your partner signal they need help? What should you do or not do?

Escalation plan: If initial interventions don't work, what's next? Calling a support person? Crisis line? Therapy session?

Safety measures: If there's any risk of self-harm, what precautions are in place? Who should be contacted?

Recovery protocol: After a crisis, what supports recovery? Rest, food, gentle activity, next-day therapy appointment?

Having this written down means you're not trying to think clearly in the middle of chaos. The decisions are already made.

16.10 Moving Forward

Preparation reduces crisis. The more you understand your partner's triggers and have plans in place, the less you'll be caught off guard.

Some accommodation is loving; excessive accommodation is harmful. Finding the balance between supporting your partner and enabling avoidance requires ongoing attention.

Your partner should be involved in planning, not just protected. Trigger management is a collaborative effort. They're the expert on their own experience. Your role is to support their capacity, not substitute for it.

Chapter 17.0 Secondary Traumatic Stress

Jessamine couldn't understand why she was having nightmares about things that had never happened to her. She'd never been abused as a child. But after three years of hearing her partner Benedictus's trauma, after countless nights holding him through flashbacks, after absorbing the details of horrors she couldn't unhear, her own sleep became haunted. She found herself hypervigilant in public, scanning for threats that weren't there. She'd lost her optimism, her sense that the world was basically safe. When her therapist used the term "secondary traumatic stress," something clicked. Her pain wasn't weakness. It was an occupational hazard of loving someone with trauma.

17.1 What Secondary Traumatic Stress Is

Secondary traumatic stress (STS) is a condition that affects people who are exposed to another person's trauma. It's not just being sad about what your partner went through. It's developing your own trauma-like symptoms from the indirect exposure (Figley, 1995).

This happens because of how human nervous systems work. We are wired for connection and empathy. When someone we love is suffering, our own nervous system responds. We co-regulate with those close to us, sharing emotional states. This is usually a good thing. It's how we comfort each other and feel connected.

But when the emotional states being shared are traumatic terror, helplessness, and horror, and when this sharing happens repeatedly over time, the helper's nervous system can become altered. The trauma becomes, in a sense, contagious.

STS is well-documented in professionals who work with trauma: therapists, first responders, emergency room staff, child protective workers (Bride et al., 2004). What's less recognized is that intimate partners are at even greater risk. You spend more time with the traumatized person than any professional. The exposure is more intense and more sustained. And the emotional stakes are higher.

17.2 Signs You May Have STS

STS can manifest in ways similar to PTSD itself:

Hypervigilance about your partner's state. You're constantly monitoring their mood, watching for signs of distress, anticipating triggers. You can't relax because you're always on alert.

Intrusive thoughts about their trauma. Even when you're not with your partner, thoughts about what happened to them intrude into your mind. You may have vivid mental images of events you didn't witness.

Emotional exhaustion and numbness. You've used up your emotional capacity. You feel flat, empty, or unable to access feelings that used to come easily.

Changes in worldview. Your sense that the world is safe and people are basically good has eroded. You've become more cynical, pessimistic, or fearful.

Physical symptoms. Sleep problems, headaches, digestive issues, fatigue, lowered immune function. The body keeps score for partners too.

Social withdrawal. You've pulled back from friendships and activities. It's too hard to explain your life to people who don't understand. It's easier to stay home.

Avoidance behaviors. You may find yourself avoiding certain topics, places, or situations that remind you of your partner's trauma.

Difficulty experiencing positive emotions. Joy, hope, and excitement feel inaccessible. There's a gray quality to life.

17.3 STS, Compassion Fatigue, Burnout

These terms are sometimes used interchangeably, but they describe related but distinct experiences.

Secondary traumatic stress refers specifically to trauma symptoms that develop from exposure to another's trauma. The symptoms mirror PTSD: intrusive thoughts, avoidance, changes in arousal and reactivity.

Compassion fatigue is a broader term that includes STS but also encompasses the emotional depletion that comes from caring over time. It's the wearing down of your capacity to care.

Burnout is characterized by exhaustion, cynicism, and reduced effectiveness, usually in response to chronic workplace stress. It can happen in any demanding situation, not just trauma-related ones.

A partner of someone with C-PTSD might experience all three: STS from the trauma exposure, compassion fatigue from the ongoing emotional demands, and burnout from the sheer relentlessness of the caregiving role.

17.4 Why Partners Are At Risk

Several factors make partners of C-PTSD survivors particularly vulnerable to STS:

Intensity of exposure. You're not seeing your partner for a fifty-minute therapy session once a week. You're living with them, sleeping next to them, present for flashbacks and nightmares, hearing details over years.

Emotional investment. Unlike a professional who maintains therapeutic distance, you're in love with this person. Their pain is your pain in a very direct way.

Lack of training. Therapists receive education on trauma and supervision to process their reactions. Partners get no such preparation.

Absence of clear boundaries. Professionals have session endings, office doors, and ethical guidelines that create separation. Partners have no such structures.

Responsibility without authority. You feel responsible for your partner's wellbeing but can't actually fix what's wrong. This helplessness is itself traumatizing.

Isolation. You may not be able to talk about your experience with others due to privacy concerns or simply because no one understands.

Duration. This isn't a time-limited exposure. It's years, potentially decades.

17.5 Risk Factors For STS

Certain factors increase vulnerability to developing STS:

Personal trauma history. If you have your own unresolved trauma, exposure to your partner's trauma can activate your own wounds.

Lack of social support. Isolated partners without outside relationships are more vulnerable.

Poor self-care practices. Neglecting your own physical and mental health reduces resilience.

High empathy. Ironically, being deeply empathic (a wonderful quality in a partner) increases risk.

Insufficient boundaries. Partners who merge completely with their loved one's experience are more likely to absorb that experience.

Longer duration of exposure. The longer you've been in the caregiving role, the higher the risk.

More severe trauma in your partner. The more intense the trauma you're exposed to, the greater the impact.

17.6 The Guilt Problem

One of the cruelest aspects of STS is the guilt that comes with acknowledging it.

Your partner is the one who experienced the trauma. They're the one suffering directly. How can you claim to be struggling when they have it so much worse?

This thinking keeps many partners from getting help. They minimize their own pain, compare unfavorably to their partner, and feel selfish for having needs.

But here's the reality: your pain doesn't compete with your partner's pain. Both can be real simultaneously. Acknowledging your struggle doesn't take anything away from them. And failing to address your STS doesn't help anyone.

Consider Apollonia, who spent two years ignoring her own symptoms because she felt guilty acknowledging pain when her partner Osric had "real" trauma. By the time she finally sought help, she was severely depressed and their relationship was suffering. Getting her own treatment ultimately helped both of them.

17.7 Self Assessment Questions

Consider these questions honestly:

Do you find yourself constantly worried about your partner's emotional state?

Have you had nightmares or intrusive images related to their trauma?

Do you feel emotionally numb or unable to experience joy?

Has your view of the world become more negative since being with your partner?

Are you experiencing physical symptoms like sleep problems, fatigue, or frequent illness?

Have you withdrawn from friends, family, or activities you used to enjoy?

Do you avoid certain topics, places, or situations because they remind you of your partner's trauma?

Do you feel hopeless about the future?

Have you lost your sense of meaning or purpose?

Do you feel constantly exhausted?

If you answered yes to several of these questions, you may be experiencing secondary traumatic stress. This isn't a diagnosis, but it's a signal to take your own wellbeing seriously.

17.8 What Helps With STS

Addressing secondary traumatic stress requires intentional action:

Acknowledge what's happening. Stop minimizing your experience. Your pain is real and deserves attention.

Get your own therapy. This is the most important intervention. A therapist who understands trauma can help you process what you've absorbed.

Create boundaries around trauma exposure. This doesn't mean abandoning your partner. It means having limits on when and how you hear about trauma, and having spaces that are protected from trauma content.

Maintain connections outside the relationship. You need people who see you as more than a caregiver, who know you as a whole person.

Practice active self-care. Sleep, exercise, nutrition, time in nature, activities that bring joy. These aren't optional.

Process your experience. Write, talk to a therapist, join a support group. The absorbed trauma needs somewhere to go.

Monitor your symptoms. Track how you're doing over time. If things are getting worse, escalate your interventions.

17.9 The Ongoing Challenge

STS isn't something you address once and then forget about. As long as you're in relationship with a trauma survivor, you're at risk for ongoing exposure effects.

Think of it like an occupational hazard that requires continuous management. Athletes take care of their bodies to prevent injury. Trauma partners need to take care of their nervous systems to prevent STS from derailing them.

This isn't fair. You didn't sign up to be traumatized by association. But it is reality. And facing that reality allows you to take protective action rather than being blindsided.

17.10 What You Learned

Your pain is real and valid. Secondary traumatic stress is a documented condition, not weakness or selfishness.

Acknowledging STS is not abandoning your partner. Taking care of yourself makes you more capable of supporting them.

You need support too. Therapy, support groups, and self-care practices are essential, not optional.

Chapter 18.0 Boundaries for Sustainability

For the first two years, Honora had no boundaries with Remigius. When he needed to talk at 3 AM, she listened. When his flashback interrupted her work call, she dropped everything. When he raged at her during emotional storms, she absorbed it. She thought this was what love meant: total availability, infinite patience, complete self-sacrifice. Then she collapsed. Panic attacks. Crying jags. A deepening resentment she couldn't shake. Her therapist gently pointed out: "You've abandoned yourself to care for him. And now there's no you left to give." Learning boundaries didn't come naturally. But slowly, Honora discovered that saying no didn't mean she loved Remigius less. It meant she could keep loving him longer.

18.1 What Boundaries Actually Are

Boundaries are the limits you set about what you will and won't do, what you will and won't accept in how you're treated. They're about your behavior, not controlling someone else's.

Boundaries are not punishments. Setting a boundary isn't the same as punishing your partner for bad behavior. It's not "I'm leaving because you need to suffer consequences." It's "I'm leaving because I need to protect myself."

Boundaries are not ultimatums. An ultimatum says "If you do X, I'll do Y" as a threat to change the other person's behavior. A boundary says "When X happens, I need to do Y for myself" regardless of whether it changes anything.

Boundaries are not about controlling your partner. You cannot control what your partner does. You can only control what you do. Boundaries focus on your actions, not on managing theirs.

Boundaries are statements of self-care. They communicate what you need to be okay. They're acts of self-respect, not acts of rejection.

18.2 Why Partners Struggle

Partners of C-PTSD survivors often have particular difficulty with boundaries for several reasons:

Fear of triggering. You know that boundaries might cause your partner distress. Setting limits might send them into a flashback or reinforce their abandonment fears. So you don't set limits, trying to prevent their pain.

Guilt about having needs. Your partner has trauma. You don't (or your trauma seems less severe). How can you claim needs when they're suffering so much? The comparison makes your own needs feel selfish.

Their fawn response makes it seem unnecessary. If your partner is a fawn type (see Chapter 8.0), they may be so accommodating that it seems like you never need boundaries. But this can mask an unsustainable dynamic where your needs are never explicitly addressed.

Not wanting to be "like" the abusers. Your partner's original trauma may have involved control, domination, or rigid rules. You don't want to replicate anything that feels like that. So you become boundaryless, the opposite extreme.

Confusing love with self-sacrifice. Cultural messages about love often emphasize complete devotion and putting the other first. Boundaries can feel like evidence of insufficient love.

18.3 Essential Partner Boundaries

Certain boundaries are necessary for your survival in this relationship:

Time for yourself. You cannot be available 24/7. You need time when you are not responsible for your partner's emotional state. This might be an hour a day, an evening a week, or a regular activity that's just yours.

Limits on emotional labor. You can be supportive, but you cannot be your partner's only source of support. There are limits on how much you can process, how late you can be kept awake, how many crisis conversations you can have in a row.

Refusal to accept abuse. Trauma may explain certain behaviors. It does not excuse abuse. If your partner is verbally attacking you, physically threatening you, or treating you with consistent contempt, that's not something you have to accept, regardless of its origins.

Maintaining other relationships. Your partner may prefer you all to themselves. That's not healthy for either of you. You need friends, family, and connections that exist independently of the relationship.

Physical safety. This is non-negotiable. If you are ever physically unsafe, you have the right and responsibility to remove yourself from that situation.

Privacy in certain areas. You may decide that certain topics, times, or spaces are protected. Maybe you don't discuss heavy trauma content after 10 PM. Maybe your work life stays separate from relationship processing.

18.4 How To Set Boundaries

Setting boundaries with a traumatized partner requires care, but it can be done:

Be clear and calm. State what you need simply, without excessive explanation or apology. "I need to go to sleep now" not "I'm so sorry, I know you need to talk, but I'm just so tired, and I have that thing tomorrow, and..."

Use "I" statements focused on your needs. "I need to take a break from this conversation" rather than "You're being too much right now."

Follow through consistently. A boundary you don't keep is just noise. If you say you're going to leave the room when voices are raised, actually leave the room. Every time.

Allow your partner's feelings without changing the boundary. They may be upset. That's okay. You can acknowledge their feelings while still maintaining your limit. "I can see this is hard for you. I still need to take this evening for myself."

Don't over-explain or justify. Long explanations invite debate. The boundary stands because you need it, not because you've constructed an airtight argument for it.

Prepare for pushback. Your partner may test boundaries, especially at first. This isn't necessarily manipulation. It may be anxiety, confusion, or simply old patterns. Stay consistent.

18.5 When Boundaries Feel Like Abandonment

For someone with C-PTSD, particularly if their trauma involved abandonment or inconsistent care, your boundaries may feel terrifying.

"I need some time alone" may translate in their trauma brain as "I'm leaving you forever."

"I can't talk about this right now" may translate as "I don't care about your pain."

"I'm going out with friends tonight" may translate as "You're not important to me."

Understanding this helps you respond with compassion while still maintaining the boundary:

Acknowledge their fear. "I know it's scary when I need space. That makes sense given what you've been through."

Reassure about the relationship. "I'm not going anywhere. I love you. And I also need this time."

Don't collapse the boundary. Acknowledging their fear doesn't mean giving up what you need. Both things can be true.

Be consistent over time. The more you reliably return, keep your word, and maintain connection alongside boundaries, the more their nervous system will learn that boundaries don't mean abandonment.

Berenice found that giving Cyril specific information helped: "I'm going to be at yoga until 7:30, then I'll be home. You can text me if you need to, and I'll respond during my break." The specificity reduced his anxiety more than vague reassurance ever had.

18.6 Boundary Language Examples

Here are some scripts for common boundary situations:

Limiting late-night conversations: "I care about what you're going through. I also need to sleep to function tomorrow. Can we continue this in the morning?"

Taking space after conflict: "I need to step away for a bit to calm down. I'm not abandoning the conversation. I'll be back in an hour."

Protecting work time: "When I'm working, I need to focus. Let's plan a time this evening when I can give you my full attention."

Declining to absorb a crisis: "I can see you're really struggling right now. I'm not able to support you through this one. Can you call your therapist or a crisis line?"

Setting limits on verbal attacks: "I want to hear you, and I'm not able to listen when you're speaking to me that way. Let me know when you're ready to talk more calmly."

Maintaining outside relationships: "I'm going to meet Nephele for dinner on Thursday. I know it's hard when I'm gone. I'll be home by 9."

18.7 When Your Partner Resists

Resistance to boundaries is normal, especially initially. Here's what might happen and how to respond:

They become more distressed. This can feel like evidence that the boundary is wrong. It's not. Their distress is understandable, and you still need the boundary. Both are true.

They accuse you of not caring. This is the trauma talking. You can say: "I understand it feels that way. I do care. And I still need this."

They test the boundary repeatedly. Consistency is your only tool here. Every time you maintain the boundary, you teach them it's real. Every time you collapse it, you teach them pushing works.

They escalate to crisis. This is manipulation if intentional, but it may also be genuine dysregulation triggered by the boundary. Either way, don't reward escalation by abandoning your limit. Get help if needed (theirs or yours), but don't teach them that crisis overrides boundaries.

Over time, something interesting often happens. Partners who initially resisted boundaries begin to feel more secure because of them. The predictability of your limits creates safety. They learn what they can count on because they know what the rules are.

18.8 Boundaries Protect The Relationship

Here's what partners often miss: boundaries aren't just for you. They're for the relationship.

Without boundaries, you burn out. When you burn out, you become resentful, withdrawn, or emotionally absent. You may eventually leave entirely.

With boundaries, you can sustain. You maintain enough of yourself to keep showing up. The relationship has the resources it needs to continue.

Think of it this way: if you give everything you have until you collapse, the relationship loses you. If you protect your capacity through boundaries, the relationship keeps you longer.

Theodora put it this way: "I used to think boundaries meant I loved Gawain less. Now I understand they mean I can keep loving him at all."

18.9 Essential Points

Boundaries are not abandonment. They're sustainability. Without them, you can't continue in the relationship long-term.

Your partner may initially struggle with boundaries, then benefit from them. Resistance at first doesn't mean boundaries are wrong. Consistency teaches new patterns.

Boundaries protect the relationship, not just you. The relationship needs you intact. Boundaries keep you intact.

Chapter 19.0 Building Support Networks

When Leocadia first started dating Ivo, she told all her friends about him. Then his C-PTSD became more apparent, and she stopped talking. It felt like a betrayal to share his struggles. It felt embarrassing to admit how hard her life had become. One by one, friendships faded. She was too tired for plans she'd once loved. She had nothing to talk about except her relationship, and she couldn't talk about that. By year three, she was completely isolated. It took a medical scare (her own) to wake her up. In the hospital, she realized there was no one to call. She'd let everyone go. Recovery started with a single text to an old friend: "I've been going through something hard. Can we talk?"

19.1 Why Isolation Fails Everyone

Isolated caregiving doesn't work. It doesn't work for professional caregivers, and it doesn't work for partners. The human nervous system isn't designed to bear that kind of load alone.

Isolation fails you because you need support that your partner cannot provide. You need people to talk to who aren't involved in the situation. You need breaks from the intensity. You need relationships that don't revolve around trauma.

Isolation fails your partner because they become your entire world, which is too much pressure. They may feel guilty for consuming your whole life. They may feel responsible for your wellbeing in ways that burden rather than help.

Isolation fails the relationship because it creates fragility. When one thing goes wrong, there's no buffer. All eggs are in one basket. Resilience requires a broader base.

Research consistently shows that social support is protective against stress and improves outcomes in difficult situations (Cohen & Wills, 1985). This applies to you as much as to your partner.

19.2 Friends Who Understand

Not everyone can be a support for this particular challenge. Some friends will minimize your experience. Others will catastrophize. Many simply won't understand what you're dealing with.

Look for friends who have capacity for complexity, people who can hold both the difficulty and the love without needing to fix or simplify. They might have their own experience with mental health challenges (theirs or someone close to them). They might simply be the kind of person who can sit with hard things.

Test the waters gradually. You don't have to share everything at once. Offer a small piece of your experience and see how they respond. Do they listen without judgment? Do they ask thoughtful questions? Do they avoid advice-giving unless you ask?

Be willing to educate. Friends who care about you may want to understand but lack knowledge about C-PTSD. Sharing this book or other resources can help them grasp what you're dealing with.

Accept imperfect support. Not every friend needs to fully understand trauma. Some can offer distraction and fun. Some can provide practical help. Different friends serve different functions.

19.3 Family Who Can Help

Family relationships around this issue can be tricky, especially if your partner's trauma involves family or if your own family doesn't understand mental health.

Identify family members who are safe. Not everyone qualifies. Look for relatives who are accepting, non-judgmental, and able to respect privacy.

Set expectations clearly. Family may want more information than you can share. They may have opinions about your relationship. Decide in advance what you will and won't discuss.

Educate selectively. Some family members can learn about C-PTSD and become better supports. Others will never get it. Spend your educational energy where it has potential.

Accept practical help. Family may be able to provide tangible support even if emotional support is limited: childcare, meals, financial help, or simply a place to stay if you need a break.

Protect your partner's privacy. Your family doesn't necessarily need to know the details of your partner's trauma. Be thoughtful about what you share and why.

19.4 Support Groups For Partners

Support groups specifically for partners of trauma survivors can be invaluable because everyone understands.

Online communities provide accessibility for those without local options. Forums, Facebook groups, and Reddit communities offer spaces to share experiences with people who get it. Be cautious about advice quality and find moderated spaces.

In-person groups offer deeper connection but may be harder to find. Look for groups through community mental health centers, trauma-focused therapy practices, or organizations serving specific populations (like partners of veterans).

What you gain from groups includes: normalization of your experience, practical strategies from others who've faced similar challenges, reduced isolation, and a space where you don't have to explain the basics.

Melisande found an online support group for partners of C-PTSD survivors that changed her life: "Finally, people who didn't look at me like I was crazy when I described my relationship. People who knew exactly what I meant by 'emotional flashback' without me having to explain. It was like coming home."

19.5 Your Own Therapist

This deserves emphasis: getting your own therapist is not optional. It's essential.

Your own therapist provides a space that's just for you. Not for processing your partner's trauma, not for getting advice on how to help them, but for attending to your own mental health.

You may need therapy to address: secondary traumatic stress, grief about the relationship you expected versus what you have, developing boundaries, processing your own emotions that don't get expressed at home, and any personal history that's being activated by your partner's trauma.

Find a therapist who understands trauma and relationships. You want someone who won't immediately tell you to leave but also won't collude with martyrdom. Look for nuanced understanding of what it means to love someone with C-PTSD.

Keep this space protected. Don't let therapy become just another place you talk about your partner. Make sure your own needs get air time.

19.6 Talking About C-PTSD With Others

Sharing about your partner's condition requires balancing authenticity with privacy.

What to consider sharing: That your partner has a trauma history affecting your relationship. That you're going through a challenging time. Enough context that people understand why you might cancel plans or seem stressed.

149

What to keep private: Specific details of your partner's trauma (unless they've consented to sharing). Information that could identify them. Anything that feels like gossip rather than seeking support.

Frame things in terms of your experience. "I'm in a challenging caregiving role" or "I'm supporting a partner through mental health treatment" respects their privacy while communicating your need.

Handle unhelpful advice gracefully. People will tell you to leave, try harder, look on the bright side, or otherwise offer input you didn't ask for. A simple "Thanks, I'll think about that" allows you to move on.

19.7 When Your Partner Resists

Some partners with C-PTSD become anxious or upset when you build outside support.

They may fear abandonment. Your connections with others may trigger worries that you'll leave them for someone easier.

They may feel exposed. Knowing you're talking about the relationship, even without details, can feel threatening.

They may worry about judgment. They're likely already carrying shame. The idea of others knowing their struggles can increase that shame.

How to address this: Reassure them that outside support helps you show up better for them. Explain that you need this to sustain yourself. Be clear about what you do and don't share. Don't ask permission (you have a right to support), but do communicate with compassion.

Most partners, after initial resistance, come to appreciate that you're taking care of yourself. It takes pressure off them and signals that you're committed for the long haul.

19.8 Maintaining Friendships

Caregiving demands can erode friendships through simple logistics: you're too tired, too busy, or too emotionally depleted for social plans.

Protect certain connections. Choose a few relationships that matter most and prioritize maintaining them, even when it's hard.

Be honest when you need to decline. "I'm going through a tough time and can't make it tonight" is better than repeated excuses that damage trust.

Accept that some friendships may not survive. Not everyone can handle your changed circumstances. That's painful, and it's also information about the limits of those connections.

Look for low-demand ways to stay connected. A text exchange, a quick coffee, or a walk together may be more sustainable than elaborate plans.

Let friends help in concrete ways. People often want to do something. Let them bring dinner, run an errand, or provide childcare. Accepting help is a form of connection.

19.9 Professional Resources

Beyond personal support, professional resources exist for partners:

Therapists specializing in trauma and relationships can provide guidance tailored to your situation.

Couples therapists (trauma-informed) can help you and your partner together, as we'll discuss in Chapter 22.0.

Support organizations like NAMI (National Alliance on Mental Illness) offer resources for family members of those with mental health conditions.

Crisis lines are available when things become urgent. Having numbers saved in your phone means you don't have to search during a crisis.

Books and educational materials (including this one) help you understand what you're dealing with and normalize your experience.

19.10 The Bottom Line

Isolation is dangerous for you and the relationship. You cannot sustain this alone. Building support isn't optional.

You need people who understand, or at least people willing to try. Not everyone will get it. Find the ones who can.

Your support network is not a betrayal of your partner. Getting help for yourself ultimately helps them by ensuring you can continue showing up.

Chapter 20.0 Protecting Your Mental Health

Galatea thought self-care meant bubble baths and face masks. She tried those things and felt nothing. She was too depleted to enjoy a bath, too exhausted to care about skincare. What she really needed was so much more fundamental: sleep, a meal that wasn't grabbed between crises, five minutes of not being responsible for someone else's emotional state. The generic wellness advice felt like a cruel joke when she was running on empty just trying to get through each day. Real self-care, she eventually learned, wasn't about pampering. It was about survival.

20.1 Why Generic Advice Fails

Most self-care content assumes you have time, energy, and mental space. Partners of C-PTSD survivors often have none of these.

"Take a relaxing bath" assumes you won't be interrupted by a crisis.

"Practice gratitude journaling" assumes you have access to positive emotions.

"Exercise regularly" assumes energy that's been depleted by hypervigilance.

"Meet friends for coffee" assumes friendships you've managed to maintain.

This doesn't mean self-care is impossible. It means the standard advice needs adapting for your actual circumstances.

The self-care that works for trauma partners is often smaller, more flexible, and more focused on basic survival than on luxury.

20.2 Micro Practices For Hard Days

On days when everything is overwhelming, micro-practices can provide tiny moments of relief:

The one-minute pause. Close your eyes for sixty seconds. Breathe. That's it. You can find one minute.

The walk to the mailbox. Getting outside, even briefly, shifts something in the nervous system. Just to the mailbox and back counts.

The single stretch. Stand up, reach your arms overhead, hold for ten seconds. Release. You've moved your body.

The glass of water. Dehydration worsens everything. Drink one glass of water consciously, tasting it.

The three breaths. Before walking into a difficult situation, take three intentional breaths. Not to feel great, just to shift slightly.

These aren't transformative. They're not supposed to be. They're survival tools for the hardest days.

20.3 Scheduled Respite

You need regular, protected time away from the caregiving role. Not when crisis permits, but scheduled in advance.

This might be: An hour daily that's yours. An evening weekly when you do something unrelated to your partner. A weekend monthly (if you can arrange it) for real rest. An annual retreat or trip for deeper restoration.

Schedule it like any other non-negotiable appointment. Don't treat it as "if everything is calm." It happens regardless.

Arrange coverage if needed. Your partner may need someone else available during your respite times. Plan this in advance.

Don't use respite time for errands. This is not when you catch up on housework. This is protected time for restoration.

Let go of guilt. Your partner survived before you. They can manage without you for an hour, an evening, a weekend. And you cannot manage without breaks.

20.4 Identity Beyond Caregiver

When caregiving becomes your entire identity, you disappear.

Maintain interests that have nothing to do with your partner or trauma. Hobbies, creative pursuits, learning new things, physical activities you enjoy. These are not frivolous. They're how you stay a person.

Connect with parts of yourself that existed before this relationship. What did you care about? What made you laugh? What dreams did you have? Those parts of you still exist, even if buried.

Be careful of complete merger. In intimate relationships, some blending is normal. Complete fusion where you have no separate self is unhealthy for both of you.

Berenice realized she hadn't read a book in two years. She used to love reading. She'd given it up because her attention was always on her partner Marius. Taking back that simple pleasure was an act of reclaiming herself.

20.5 Physical Health Often Neglected

Chronic stress takes a physical toll. Partners often neglect their bodies while attending to their partner's mental health.

Sleep is foundational. Everything is harder without adequate sleep. Protect your sleep as fiercely as you protect your partner from triggers. If their nightmares disrupt your sleep, consider sleeping separately sometimes.

Nutrition matters. Stress eating, skipping meals, or surviving on caffeine and convenience food depletes your resources. You don't need a perfect diet, but you need to eat actual food.

Movement helps regulate the nervous system. This doesn't have to be gym workouts. Walking, stretching, dancing in your kitchen, anything that moves your body.

Medical care shouldn't be postponed. Keep your own doctor's appointments. Address health issues. You're no good to anyone if you're sick.

Substances require honesty. Alcohol, drugs, or medication misuse can creep in as coping mechanisms. Notice if your use is increasing.

20.6 Spiritual And Meaning Making

For some partners, spiritual practices or meaning-making frameworks provide essential support.

This might look like: Religious practice if you're religious. Meditation or mindfulness. Time in nature. Connection to something larger than your immediate circumstances. Philosophical or existential reflection on suffering and purpose.

Meaning-making helps with the "why." When you're in the hardest moments, having some framework for understanding why this matters, why you're doing this, what purpose it serves, can sustain you.

This is personal territory. What works for one person feels hollow to another. Find what resonates for you.

20.7 Managing Difficult Emotions

Partners carry feelings that don't get much airtime. Acknowledging them is part of self-care.

Grief for the relationship you expected. Most people don't plan to partner with someone who has severe trauma. Grieving the easier relationship you imagined is legitimate and necessary.

Anger that feels forbidden. Caregivers often suppress anger because it seems unkind. But anger at the situation, at the unfairness, even at your partner sometimes, is natural. Finding safe places to express it prevents it from corroding you.

Hopelessness that needs attention. If you're losing hope that things will improve, that's a signal. It may mean you need more support, or it may mean something needs to change in the relationship.

Joy that feels disloyal. Some partners feel guilty experiencing happiness when their loved one is struggling. But joy isn't betrayal. You're allowed to experience good things.

20.8 Warning Signs

Watch for these signs that you need more support than you're getting:

Persistent depression or anxiety that isn't lifting.

Physical symptoms without medical explanation (or with causes linked to stress).

Reliance on substances to get through.

Thoughts of self-harm or hopelessness.

Complete loss of interest in things you used to enjoy.

Inability to function in other areas of life (work, other relationships).

Increasing resentment toward your partner that you can't shake.

Thoughts about leaving the relationship that consume you.

These signs don't mean you're weak or failing. They mean the load is too heavy for the resources you have. More support is needed.

20.9 Joy Is Not Selfish

Here's something partners need to hear: experiencing joy is not selfish.

Your happiness doesn't take away from your partner's healing. Your pleasure doesn't mean you don't care about their pain. Your laughter in the midst of hard times is not inappropriate.

In fact, your positive experiences help the relationship. They model that life can include good things. They give you energy to bring back into caregiving. They remind both of you what you're working toward.

Give yourself permission to feel good. To laugh. To enjoy. Even while hard things are happening. Life contains both.

20.10 Your Action Steps

Self-care is not selfish. It's essential. Without it, you cannot sustain yourself or your relationship.

You can't pour from an empty cup. This cliché exists because it's true. Your partner needs you to have something left to give.

Your wellbeing benefits your partner too. Taking care of yourself isn't in competition with taking care of them. It's what makes caring for them possible.

Chapter 21.0 Supporting Their Healing

Faustina wanted so badly to fix Darian. She researched treatment modalities obsessively. She suggested therapists, recommended books, forwarded articles. She tracked his symptoms and reported them to him weekly. When his therapy seemed to be stalling, she called his therapist (without his knowledge) to give "additional information." It wasn't until the therapist gently suggested that Faustina was crossing lines that she realized: her helping had become hindering. She wasn't Darian's treatment team. She was his partner. And those are very different roles.

21.1 Evidence Based Treatments

Understanding what treatments work for C-PTSD helps you support your partner's healing journey knowledgeably.

Trauma-focused therapy approaches directly address traumatic memories and their effects. EMDR (Eye Movement Desensitization and Reprocessing) uses bilateral stimulation while processing traumatic memories and has strong evidence for PTSD (Shapiro, 2018). CPT (Cognitive Processing Therapy) focuses on how trauma has affected thinking patterns. PE (Prolonged Exposure) involves gradual, repeated exposure to trauma-related memories and situations.

Attachment-based approaches address the relational wounds central to C-PTSD. These therapies prioritize the therapeutic relationship as a vehicle for healing attachment patterns.

Somatic therapies address trauma held in the body. Somatic Experiencing helps discharge trapped survival energy. Sensorimotor Psychotherapy integrates body-based interventions with talk therapy.

Internal Family Systems (IFS) works with different "parts" of the personality, including traumatized parts and protective parts. It's particularly effective for complex trauma (Schwartz, 2021).

Schema Therapy addresses deeply held patterns (schemas) that developed from childhood experiences, combining cognitive, behavioral, and experiential approaches.

DBT (Dialectical Behavior Therapy) teaches emotion regulation, distress tolerance, and interpersonal skills. While developed for borderline personality disorder, it's helpful for anyone struggling with emotional dysregulation.

21.2 Supporting Without Becoming Therapist

Your role is partner, not treatment provider. Understanding the difference protects both of you.

Encouraging without pushing means expressing support for their healing efforts without pressuring them about specifics. "I'm glad you're working with your therapist" is different from "You should ask your therapist about EMDR next session."

Tolerating the "worse before better" phase acknowledges that trauma therapy often stirs things up before settling them down. Your partner may be more symptomatic during active processing. This is normal, not evidence that therapy isn't working.

Not asking for play-by-play means respecting the privacy of their therapy. What happens in sessions is between them and their therapist. You don't need to know every detail.

Supporting between-session practices might include encouraging them to do their therapy homework, creating space for grounding exercises, or practicing communication skills together when invited.

21.3 When They Resist Treatment

Some partners refuse to engage in treatment, which puts you in a difficult position.

Reasons for resistance include: fear of revisiting trauma, shame about needing help, previous bad experiences with therapy, skepticism about whether it can help, or practical barriers like cost and time.

What you can do: Express your concerns lovingly. Share how their untreated trauma affects you and the relationship. Offer to help with logistics (finding therapists, managing insurance, providing transportation). Normalize therapy as a tool for everyone, not evidence of being broken.

What you can't do: Make them go. Force change. Fix them yourself. Take responsibility for their healing.

At some point, if they persistently refuse treatment while you suffer the consequences, that becomes a relationship issue. See Chapter 24.0 for when love isn't enough.

21.4 Red Flags In Treatment

Not all therapy is good therapy. Watch for warning signs:

Therapist seems to be making things worse over time, not just temporarily. Some activation is normal, but persistent deterioration isn't.

Therapist encourages dependence rather than building your partner's capacity.

Therapist dismisses your partner's concerns or minimizes their experience.

Therapy has no direction or goals, even after many sessions.

Therapist shares inappropriate personal information or has boundary problems.

Your partner feels worse about themselves (not just their trauma) after sessions.

Therapist speaks disparagingly about you or the relationship without knowing you.

If you notice these signs, gently raising concerns with your partner is appropriate. The final decision is theirs, but your observations matter.

21.5 Medication Considerations

Medication is often part of C-PTSD treatment. What partners should know:

Medication can help with symptoms like depression, anxiety, sleep problems, and hyperarousal. It doesn't cure C-PTSD but can make other treatment more accessible.

Finding the right medication takes time. There may be a trial period with side effects or ineffective medications before finding what works.

Side effects may affect the relationship. Sexual side effects, emotional numbing, fatigue, or other changes can impact your partnership.

Medication decisions belong to your partner and their prescriber. Your input matters, but you're not the decision-maker.

Support adherence without policing. Encourage them to take medication as prescribed, but don't become the pill police.

21.6 Questions For Therapists

When your partner is seeking a therapist, these questions help assess fit:

What is your experience treating Complex PTSD or developmental trauma?

What approaches do you use? Are they evidence-based?

How do you work with the body, or do you focus primarily on talk?

What does treatment typically look like? How long? What phases?

How do you involve partners? (Some involvement is good; too much may indicate boundary issues.)

What training do you have in trauma-informed care?

21.7 The Partner's Proper Role

Here's a clear delineation:

Your job is to: Be a loving, consistent presence. Provide a safe relationship environment. Support their treatment engagement. Take care of yourself so you can sustain this. Give feedback about how things affect you.

Their therapist's job is to: Provide expert trauma treatment. Process traumatic memories. Teach skills and coping strategies. Challenge unhelpful patterns. Maintain appropriate boundaries.

The overlap is minimal. You are not a co-therapist. Resist the urge to implement therapeutic interventions at home unless specifically guided by their treatment provider.

21.8 What You Learned

You can support without directing. Your role is partner, not therapist. Stay in your lane while cheering from the sidelines.

Treatment is your partner's responsibility, not yours. You can encourage, but you can't make them heal.

The right therapist makes an enormous difference. A good fit can transform recovery. A bad fit can cause harm.

Chapter 22.0 Couples Therapy for Trauma

Nephele thought couples therapy would save her relationship with Quirin. The therapist they found seemed competent enough. But session after session, things got worse. The therapist kept pushing them to "communicate feelings" in ways that triggered Quirin's shame spiral. Exercises designed to build intimacy activated his trauma. Feedback Nephele shared was used by Quirin's inner critic as ammunition for self-attack. It wasn't until they found a trauma-informed couples therapist that things began to shift. "Not all couples therapy is the same," the new therapist explained. "When trauma is involved, we need to go slower and work differently."

22.1 Why Generic Approaches Can Harm

Standard couples therapy techniques were designed for couples dealing with communication problems, not trauma.

Techniques that backfire include:

"Express your feelings openly" can overwhelm a trauma survivor and trigger shutdown.

"Look into each other's eyes and share vulnerabilities" can activate attachment terror.

"Take turns sharing grievances" can spiral into shame and defensive attacks.

"Touch each other while discussing problems" can trigger dissociation.

The problem isn't that these techniques are bad. For many couples, they're helpful. But they assume both partners have the nervous system regulation capacity to tolerate emotional intensity. C-PTSD often impairs this capacity.

A therapist who doesn't understand trauma may inadvertently retraumatize your partner and damage the relationship further.

22.2 Trauma Informed Approaches

Several couples therapy models are specifically designed for trauma:

Emotionally Focused Therapy (EFT) for trauma, developed by Susan Johnson, addresses attachment bonds and helps couples become safe havens for each other. For trauma survivors, it includes additional attention to pacing and regulation (Johnson, 2002).

Cognitive-Behavioral Conjoint Therapy for PTSD (CBCT) is a structured approach that includes both partners in treating PTSD. It addresses avoidance, communication, and trauma processing within the relationship context (Monson & Fredman, 2012).

Developmental Couples Therapy for Complex Trauma (DCTCT) specifically addresses the attachment and mentalizing difficulties that come with developmental trauma.

PACT (Psychobiological Approach to Couple Therapy) uses neuroscience and attachment theory to help couples regulate each other's nervous systems.

These approaches share common features: they go slowly, they prioritize safety and regulation, they understand trauma's impact on the brain, and they work with the relationship as a healing context rather than just a problem to fix.

22.3 When To Pursue Couples Work

Couples therapy is most appropriate when:

Both partners are relatively stable. If either partner is in active crisis, individual work should come first.

There's genuine commitment to the relationship. Couples therapy is for improving relationships, not deciding whether to stay.

No active abuse is occurring. Couples therapy should not happen alongside ongoing abuse. The abuser needs individual accountability work first.

Individual treatment is in place or accessible. Couples therapy supplements, not replaces, individual trauma treatment.

Both partners consent and want to participate. Coerced couples therapy doesn't work.

22.4 When To Wait

Couples therapy should be delayed when:

Your partner is in crisis. Severe depression, active suicidality, or acute PTSD symptoms need individual attention first.

Active addiction is present. Addiction treatment takes priority. Couples work with an actively addicted partner is usually unproductive.

Individual trauma work hasn't started. Sometimes your partner needs individual stabilization before they can tolerate the intensity of couples work.

The relationship is actively unsafe. Physical violence, threats, or severe emotional abuse need addressing through other means before couples therapy.

One partner is clearly not invested. Couples therapy requires two willing participants.

22.5 Finding The Right Therapist

Not every couples therapist can work effectively with trauma. Here's what to look for:

Training in trauma. Ask specifically about their training in trauma-informed approaches.

Experience with C-PTSD couples. General trauma knowledge may not be enough. Complex trauma creates specific relationship patterns.

Willingness to go slowly. A therapist who pushes for quick breakthroughs may not understand trauma's pace.

Integration with individual treatment. They should want to coordinate (with appropriate consent) with your partner's individual therapist.

Attention to both partners. A trauma-informed couples therapist won't forget that you have needs too.

Questions to ask potential therapists:

What is your approach to couples therapy when one partner has trauma history?

How do you handle it when someone becomes triggered in session?

How do you balance attention to both partners' needs?

What's your training in trauma-informed care?

How do you coordinate with individual therapists?

22.6 What To Expect

Trauma-informed couples work typically looks different from standard approaches:

Pacing is slower. You won't be pushed into intense emotional exchanges before the foundation is built.

Safety is paramount. The therapist works to ensure both partners feel safe before tackling difficult material.

Education is included. Understanding trauma's impact on the relationship is part of the work.

Regulation skills are taught. You'll both learn techniques for managing activation.

The relationship becomes a healing context. The goal isn't just resolving problems but making the relationship a secure base for both of you.

Progress may be non-linear. Expect setbacks, especially when deeper material is accessed.

22.7 Your Role In The Process

As the partner without C-PTSD (or with less severe trauma), you have a particular role:

Stay engaged even when it's hard. Couples therapy requires you to show up consistently.

Be open to feedback about your patterns. It's not all about your partner's trauma. You have contributions to the dynamic too.

Maintain your own support. Couples therapy can stir up your own stuff. Keep your individual resources in place.

Practice patience with the pace. It may feel slower than you want. Trust the process.

Communicate when something isn't working. If the therapy feels harmful, say so.

22.8 What We Covered

Not all couples therapists understand trauma. Seek out therapists with specific training and experience.

Timing matters. Sometimes individual work comes first. The relationship can wait while foundational work happens.

The relationship can be a vehicle for healing. With the right support, your partnership becomes part of the recovery process.

Chapter 23.0 Recovery Is Possible

For five years, Salome wasn't sure things would ever change. Simeon's symptoms were so persistent, so consuming. Every small improvement seemed followed by a setback. There were periods when she wondered if she was fooling herself, staying in a situation that would never get better. Then, somewhere around year six, she noticed something different. The flashbacks still came, but they were shorter. Simeon could recognize them and name them. He could comfort himself in ways he couldn't before. He reached for her during hard moments instead of pushing away. It wasn't dramatic transformation. It was incremental, almost invisible from week to week. But looking back, the change was undeniable. Her husband was still a trauma survivor. But he was also, slowly, becoming someone who could thrive.

23.1 What Recovery Means

Recovery from C-PTSD doesn't mean symptoms disappear completely. It means something more nuanced and more achievable.

Recovery means symptoms decrease in frequency and intensity. Flashbacks still happen, but less often and less severely. Triggers still exist, but they're more manageable.

Recovery means earned secure attachment becomes possible. As we discussed in Chapter 12.0, people can develop secure attachment in adulthood even if they didn't have it in childhood. This is one of the most hopeful findings in attachment research (Roisman et al., 2002).

Recovery means the inner critic quiets. It doesn't disappear, but it loses some of its power. Your partner can recognize the critic as critic rather than truth.

Recovery means emotional flashbacks become shorter and less intense. The regression still happens, but the person can often recognize it, orient to the present, and climb out faster.

Recovery means increased capacity for intimacy. The defenses that once kept love out become more permeable. Connection becomes less threatening.

23.2 The Three Stages

Trauma recovery typically moves through three phases, though not linearly (Herman, 1992):

Stage One: Safety and Stabilization. Before any trauma can be processed, the person needs to feel safe and have skills to manage overwhelming emotions. This stage focuses on building coping skills, establishing safety in therapy and life, and stabilizing any crisis symptoms. Many people spend months or years in this stage.

Stage Two: Processing Trauma. Once stabilized, the actual traumatic material can be addressed. This might involve telling the trauma story, processing specific memories through EMDR or other approaches, and making meaning of what happened. This is often the hardest phase.

Stage Three: Integration and Reconnection. After processing, the work shifts to integrating what's been learned, reconnecting with life and relationships, and building a future. Identity shifts from "trauma survivor" to "person who experienced trauma and healed."

These stages spiral rather than progress straight through. Someone might move into Stage Two, encounter material that destabilizes them, and return to Stage One work before progressing again.

23.3 Signs Of Improvement

In relationships, improvement shows up in specific ways:

Increased emotional regulation. Your partner can experience strong emotions without being completely overwhelmed. They can return to baseline more quickly after activation.

Better communication during stress. Even when triggered, they can maintain some capacity for dialogue. Repairs happen more smoothly.

Ability to repair after ruptures. Conflicts still happen, but they no longer threaten the relationship's foundation. Both of you can come back together after hard moments.

Deeper intimacy over time. The walls come down gradually. Your partner can let you in further than before.

Decreased survival response intensity. The 4F responses (Chapter 5.0-8.0) are still present but less extreme. There's more flexibility in how they respond to perceived threats.

Greater capacity to give as well as receive. Your partner can attend to your needs, not just their own trauma.

More presence in daily life. They're here, now, with you, more often than lost in the past or braced for the future.

23.4 The Non-Linear Path

Healing isn't a straight line. Setbacks are normal and don't erase progress.

Your partner may have a period of significant improvement, then encounter a new trigger or stressor that reactivates symptoms. This isn't failure. It's how healing works.

Think of it like waves on a beach. The tide is coming in (overall improvement), but individual waves still flow in and out. Sometimes a bigger wave comes further up the beach than expected. That doesn't mean the tide isn't rising.

Factors that can cause temporary setbacks include: major life stressors, trauma anniversaries, health problems, accessing deeper layers of trauma in therapy, relationship conflicts, and losses or transitions.

What matters isn't avoiding setbacks but how they're handled. Can your partner use the skills they've developed? Can they recognize what's happening? Can they reach out for support? Can they recover faster than they would have before?

23.5 Stories Of Change

Eudora and Gawain had been together for eight years when he finally started trauma therapy. The first two years of treatment were brutal. Gawain processed memories that had been buried for decades. His symptoms intensified before they improved. There were moments Eudora questioned whether therapy was helping or hurting. But by year three, something shifted. Gawain could talk about his childhood without dissociating. He could receive her love without deflecting it. He initiated affection in ways he never had before. "I feel like I'm finally meeting the real him," Eudora said. "The one who was buried under all that protection."

Theophilus spent most of his twenties in and out of treatment for what was diagnosed as depression, then anxiety, then bipolar disorder. Nothing helped because nothing addressed the actual problem: childhood trauma that had never been named. At thirty-two, he found a therapist who understood C-PTSD. The work was slow. Five years of weekly therapy. Some medication adjustment. A lot of learning to recognize flashbacks and regulate his nervous system. His partner Honora watched the transformation happen gradually. "He's not a different person," she reflected. "He's the person he always was, but without the weight crushing him. He laughs now. He can plan for the future. He doesn't expect me to leave every time we fight."

23.6 The Relationship's Role

Your relationship isn't just a bystander to your partner's recovery. It can be an active part of healing.

Research shows that secure attachment relationships help regulate the nervous system and provide corrective emotional experiences (Siegel, 2012). Every time you and your partner successfully repair a rupture, every time you provide consistent safety, every time you love them through a hard moment, you're contributing to neural rewiring.

This doesn't mean you're responsible for their healing. It means your relationship matters. It's a context in which healing becomes more possible.

The goal isn't to be their therapist. It's to be a secure base, a safe haven they can return to, a relationship that demonstrates (again and again) that intimacy doesn't have to mean danger.

23.7 Patience For The Journey

Recovery is measured in years, not months. This is important to understand from the beginning.

Complex trauma that developed over years of childhood cannot be resolved in weeks. The nervous system needs sustained safety to rewire. The attachment patterns need repeated disconfirmation to update. The inner critic needs consistent contrary evidence to quiet.

Some research suggests three to five years of treatment for significant C-PTSD improvement. Some people need longer. Very few need less.

This doesn't mean suffering for years. It means gradual, incremental improvement over time. Life can be good while healing is happening. It just won't be quick.

23.8 What We Learned

Full recovery is possible, though it looks different than "no symptoms." Your partner may always have a trauma history. What changes is how much that history controls their present.

The relationship itself can be part of healing. Your consistent presence contributes to the safety that makes recovery possible.

Patience measured in years, not months. Set your expectations for the long haul. Then be pleasantly surprised by progress along the way.

Chapter 24.0 When Love Is Not Enough

Clotilde didn't want to leave Erasmus. She'd invested eight years, witnessed his therapy, held him through countless flashbacks. But somewhere in year seven, she started having chest pains. Her hair was falling out. She'd lost twenty pounds from stress. Her therapist pointed out that she was showing signs of serious health deterioration. "At what point," the therapist asked gently, "does staying begin to harm you more than leaving would harm him?" Clotilde didn't have an answer. She loved Erasmus. And she was also disappearing. The hardest thing she ever did was finally saying: "I can love you and also not be able to live like this anymore."

24.1 Hard Versus Harmful

There's a difference between a relationship that's hard and one that's harmful.

Hard looks like: challenges, struggles, slow progress, difficult moments, exhaustion, need for support. Hard is sustainable with the right resources. Hard can be survived.

Harmful looks like: deterioration that doesn't reverse, health consequences that accumulate, abuse that continues, safety that's compromised, wellbeing that erodes beyond recovery.

Loving someone with C-PTSD is hard. That doesn't automatically make it harmful. Many partners thrive in these relationships when they have adequate support.

But sometimes, for some partners, in some situations, the relationship crosses from hard into harmful. Recognizing this line is crucial.

24.2 When Staying Becomes Untenable

Several situations may indicate that staying is no longer sustainable:

Abuse is occurring. Trauma explains behavior. It does not excuse abuse. If your partner is physically violent, consistently emotionally abusive, or treating you with sustained contempt, having a trauma history doesn't make that acceptable. You have the right to safety.

Your partner refuses to get help. If they're unwilling to engage in treatment while their symptoms devastate the relationship, you're stuck in a situation that won't change. You cannot heal them. They must choose that.

Your own health is deteriorating beyond repair. If you're developing serious physical or mental health problems from the relationship stress, your body is telling you something important.

Children are being harmed. If there are children in the relationship who are suffering from your partner's symptoms or behavior, their protection must be prioritized.

You've given everything and have nothing left. Some partners reach a point of complete depletion where they cannot continue. This isn't failure. It's honesty.

24.3 Setting Limits On Waiting

If your partner is in treatment but progress is very slow, you may need to set internal limits on how long you'll wait.

This isn't an ultimatum delivered to your partner ("Get better by June or I'm leaving"). It's a private assessment for yourself about sustainability.

Questions to ask yourself:

Can I maintain my own health and wellbeing at the current pace of change?

What would need to be different in six months for me to feel okay about continuing?

Am I seeing any improvement, even if it's slow?

Have I been saying "just a little longer" for years without any change?

What would I advise a friend in my situation?

Sometimes setting an internal timeline helps you be more patient (you know there's a limit) while also protecting you from indefinite waiting.

24.4 Leaving With Care

If you decide to leave a relationship with someone who has C-PTSD, how you do it matters.

Don't disappear suddenly. This is retraumatizing. The abandonment wound is real. A sudden vanishing, even if you feel you need to escape, does significant harm.

Be honest about your reasons without being cruel. "I love you, and I can't sustain this relationship anymore" is different from "You're too broken to love."

Allow some transition time if safely possible. Abrupt endings, while sometimes necessary for safety, are harder to process than transitions with some warning.

Encourage their continued treatment. Just because you're leaving doesn't mean they don't deserve healing. Express hope for their recovery even if you won't be there to see it.

Safety plan if needed. If there's any risk of self-harm from your partner, have supports in place. This might mean alerting their therapist (with whatever consent is possible), ensuring friends or family know, or having crisis resources available.

24.5 Leaving Without Guilt

Guilt is almost inevitable when leaving someone vulnerable. But guilt is not a reliable guide to what's right.

You are not responsible for their existence or wellbeing. They survived before you. They can survive after you. As much as they may feel they can't live without you, they can.

Staying when you're destroyed doesn't help anyone. A depleted, resentful, or disappearing partner doesn't serve your loved one's healing. Sometimes leaving is actually kinder than staying poorly.

Your life matters too. You have one life. You deserve to be healthy and happy. This isn't selfish. It's basic self-preservation.

Leaving doesn't mean their trauma was fake or unimportant. You can recognize the reality of their suffering and still conclude you can't be the one to witness it anymore.

24.6 When Staying Enables

Sometimes staying enables dysfunction rather than supporting recovery.

Signs you might be enabling:

Your partner has no motivation to change because you absorb all consequences of their symptoms.

They've stopped working on recovery because you've accommodated so completely that there's no pressure.

Your presence allows them to avoid facing their problems.

You're doing for them what they could do for themselves.

The relationship has become entirely organized around their trauma with no room for anything else.

This isn't a reason to leave necessarily. But it is a reason to examine whether your way of staying is actually helping or inadvertently maintaining the status quo.

24.7 The Middle Ground

Between staying exactly as you have been and leaving entirely, there are middle options.

Staying differently might mean: setting firmer boundaries, reducing your level of accommodation, requiring treatment engagement as a condition of continuing, separating temporarily while both of you get support, or restructuring the relationship in ways that protect you better.

Sometimes a clear statement of limits ("I can't continue unless there's treatment progress") catalyzes change. Sometimes it doesn't. But it's worth trying before complete departure.

24.8 Getting Support For The Decision

Whether you stay, leave, or try something in between, you need support for the process.

Your own therapist helps you sort through your feelings and decisions without telling you what to do.

Friends and family who can listen without judgment offer a sounding board.

Support groups for partners provide perspective from others who understand.

A couples therapist (if appropriate) might help you make the decision together or separate in a healthier way.

Don't make this decision in complete isolation. You need outside perspective and emotional support.

24.9 Essential Points

Love without limits helps no one. Boundaries, requirements, and limits are not unloving. They're necessary for sustainability.

Your wellbeing matters as much as your partner's. This isn't selfish. It's true. Your life has equal value.

Leaving can sometimes be the most loving choice. For you, for them, for whatever future each of you might have separately.

Chapter 25.0 Love as Medicine

Theodora sometimes looks back at the version of herself who met Gawain fifteen years ago and barely recognizes her. She didn't know what C-PTSD was. She didn't know what emotional flashbacks were, what the inner critic did, what disorganized attachment meant. She just knew she loved a man who was wounded in ways she couldn't see but could feel. Fifteen years later, they're still together. Gawain is healed enough to be present, connected, capable of joy. Theodora is wiser, more patient, more certain of her own boundaries. The relationship itself transformed them both. Not perfectly. Not without scars. But thoroughly. Love, it turned out, was part of the medicine. Not the whole prescription, but a crucial ingredient that no therapy could provide.

25.1 The Research On Relationship

Science confirms what you may sense intuitively: relationships can be healing contexts for trauma.

Studies show that secure attachment relationships help regulate the nervous system and provide what researchers call "corrective emotional experiences" (Johnson, 2002). This means that experiencing safety, consistency, and attunement in an adult relationship can gradually update the expectations encoded from childhood.

The brain remains plastic throughout life. Neural pathways formed in traumatic environments can be rewired through sustained new experiences. Your relationship, with its consistent safety and repeated repairs, contributes to this rewiring (Siegel, 2012).

Couples therapy research demonstrates that addressing trauma within the relationship context can reduce PTSD symptoms while improving relationship satisfaction (Monson et al., 2012). The relationship itself becomes therapeutic.

This doesn't mean love alone heals trauma. Professional treatment is essential. But love provides something treatment can't: daily evidence that relationships can be safe, repeated experiences of being seen and accepted, and a context for practicing new patterns.

25.2 What Your Love Can Do

Your love provides a secure base for healing. Attachment theory describes a secure base as someone we can turn to for comfort and support, and from whom we can venture out to explore the world (Bowlby, 1988). You can be that for your partner.

Your love models healthy relating. Every time you communicate fairly, honor boundaries, repair ruptures, and treat your partner with respect, you're demonstrating what healthy relationship looks like. This is particularly powerful for someone who never saw it growing up.

Your love witnesses transformation. Recovery is lonely work. Having someone who sees the progress, celebrates the victories, and stays present through the setbacks matters enormously.

Your love disconfirms trauma expectations. Your partner's trauma taught them that people who love them will hurt, leave, or betray them. Every day you don't do those things, you provide evidence that contradicts the old beliefs.

25.3 What Your Love Cannot Do

Your love cannot replace professional treatment. Trauma-focused therapy, done by trained professionals, is essential for processing traumatic material and developing skills. Your love is a context for healing, not a substitute for treatment.

Your love cannot undo the past. What happened to your partner happened. Nothing you do can erase it. You can help them heal, but you can't make it un-happen.

Your love cannot make healing happen faster. Recovery takes the time it takes. Your impatience, however understandable, doesn't speed things up. In fact, pressure can slow progress.

Your love cannot heal by itself. You're a crucial ingredient, not the entire recipe. Don't take it personally if your love alone isn't enough to resolve symptoms. It was never supposed to be.

25.4 Honoring Your Commitment

You made a commitment to someone who carries trauma. Whether you knew the full extent when you committed or learned it along the way, you're here now.

Honoring commitment means showing up consistently, even when it's hard. It means staying engaged through difficult periods. It means continuing to offer yourself even when your offerings seem rejected.

It does not mean sacrificing yourself entirely. Commitment is not martyrdom. The commitment to your partner exists alongside a commitment to your own wellbeing. Both must be honored.

25.5 Honoring Your Limits

You also have limits. Honoring them is not betrayal.

You are human, with finite energy, patience, and capacity. Recognizing and respecting your limits is not failure. It's realism.

Some days you won't do it well. You'll lose patience. You'll say the wrong thing. You'll need to walk away. That's okay. Perfection isn't required.

If you reach a point where continuing harms you beyond what's sustainable, that limit deserves respect too. As we discussed in Chapter 24.0, sometimes the most loving thing is acknowledging you cannot continue.

25.6 The Gift Of Choosing Each Other

There's something powerful about two people choosing each other despite the hard.

You know the difficulties. You know the challenges. You know the cost. And you're still here. That choice, renewed over time, is a profound form of love.

Your partner, too, is making a choice. They're letting you into places they've kept hidden. They're risking vulnerability despite every lesson that taught them vulnerability is dangerous. That's courage.

Together, you're building something that trauma tried to make impossible: a real relationship, imperfect but genuine, marked by struggle but also by growth.

25.7 Final Words

You are doing something incredibly hard and incredibly meaningful. Supporting a partner through C-PTSD recovery is one of the most demanding forms of love there is. Not everyone can do it. Not everyone should. But you're doing it.

Perfect support isn't required. You'll get it wrong sometimes. What matters is the overall pattern: consistent enough, safe enough, present enough over time.

There is hope. Recovery happens. Relationships survive and even thrive. Your love matters, even when it seems invisible. Even when it seems rejected. Even when you're not sure you can keep going.

Keep going anyway. One day at a time. One repair at a time. One small moment of connection at a time.

That's how healing happens.

25.8 Affirmations For The Journey

For yourself:

I can love my partner and take care of myself.

My needs matter alongside theirs.

I am doing something hard and meaningful.

I don't have to be perfect to be helpful.

My limits are not failures.

For your relationship:

We are in this together.

Ruptures can be repaired.

Progress is real, even when invisible.

Our relationship can survive difficult seasons.

Love is part of the medicine.

25.9 Moving Forward

As you close this book, carry with you what's been useful. Leave behind what doesn't fit. Use the tools and strategies when they help. Set them aside when they don't.

Keep learning. Keep getting support. Keep taking care of yourself. Keep showing up for your partner while protecting your own wellbeing.

The path ahead will have hard days. It will also have good ones. Both are part of the journey.

Thank you for caring enough to read this. Thank you for loving someone who is working to heal. Thank you for staying present in one of the most difficult forms of partnership there is.

There is hope. And you are part of making it real.

Appendix A: Quick Reference Cards

These cards can be photocopied or photographed for easy reference during difficult moments.

Card 1: Emotional Flashback First Aid

When you recognize your partner is in a flashback:

1. Stay calm yourself. Your regulation helps them.
2. Speak softly and simply. "I'm here. You're safe. This will pass."
3. Don't argue or reason. Logic isn't accessible right now.
4. Offer grounding gently. "Can you feel your feet? What do you see around you?"
5. Give space if needed. Ask: "Do you want me close or should I give you room?"
6. Wait it out. Flashbacks end. Be patient.
7. Reconnect after. Gentle presence, no immediate processing.

What NOT to do:

- Don't say "calm down" or "you're overreacting"
- Don't take it personally
- Don't demand explanations
- Don't try to fix it

Card 2: The 4F Types At A Glance

Fight: Anger, criticism, control, defensiveness *Deepest fear:* Being controlled or helpless *What helps:* Stay calm, don't escalate, set limits

Flight: Busyness, workaholism, constant activity *Deepest fear:* Stillness brings overwhelming feelings *What helps:* Join in activity, gradual presence building

Freeze: Withdrawal, dissociation, shutdown *Deepest fear:* Engagement brings annihilation *What helps:* Gentle presence, no demands, patience

Fawn: People-pleasing, no boundaries, loss of self *Deepest fear:* Having needs leads to abandonment *What helps:* Celebrate their "no," encourage authenticity

---

Card 3: Crisis De-escalation Steps

1. **Assess safety.** Is anyone at risk of harm? If yes, call for help.
2. **Lower stimulation.** Reduce noise, light, number of people.
3. **Speak calmly.** Slow, soft, short sentences.
4. **Don't touch without permission.** Ask first.
5. **Offer choices.** "Would you like water or to sit down?" Choices restore agency.
6. **Use grounding.** "Name five things you see."
7. **Wait.** Crisis states pass. Stay present.
8. **Get support after.** For them and for you.

Card 4: Self-Care Emergency Plan

When you're depleted and need immediate support:

In the next 5 minutes:

- One minute of deep breathing
- Glass of water
- Step outside briefly

In the next hour:

- Text a supportive friend
- Take a walk
- Do one nurturing thing (shower, snack, rest)

In the next day:

- Schedule therapy or call crisis support
- Get to bed early
- Reach out to your support network

Warning signs I need professional help:

- Thoughts of self-harm
- Unable to function at work or home
- Physical symptoms persisting
- Feeling hopeless for more than a few days

Card 5: When To Call For Help

Call 911 or go to emergency room if:

- Anyone is in immediate danger
- Active suicide attempt or plan
- Psychotic symptoms (break from reality)
- Violence occurring or about to occur

Call crisis line (988 in US) if:

- Suicidal thoughts without immediate plan
- Severe distress that won't resolve
- You or your partner need to talk to someone now

Contact therapist urgently if:

- Significant worsening of symptoms
- New concerning behaviors
- Need guidance on safety
- Medication concerns

Your specific emergency contacts: Partner's therapist: _____ Your therapist: _____ Trusted friend/family: _____ Crisis line: 988 (US)

Appendix B: Additional Resources

Books For Further Reading

For Partners:

Loving Someone with PTSD by Aphrodite Matsakis. Practical guide focused on PTSD generally, adaptable for C-PTSD.

When Someone You Love Suffers from Posttraumatic Stress by Claudia Zayfert and Jason DeViva. Comprehensive information for family members.

The PTSD Relationship by Diane England. Focuses on maintaining relationship health alongside PTSD.

For Understanding C-PTSD:

Complex PTSD: From Surviving to Thriving by Pete Walker. The essential guide to understanding C-PTSD from the inside.

The Body Keeps the Score by Bessel van der Kolk. Groundbreaking overview of trauma and the body.

Trauma and Recovery by Judith Herman. The foundational text on trauma, including complex trauma.

For Self-Care:

Self-Compassion by Kristin Neff. Building kindness toward yourself.

Boundaries by Henry Cloud and John Townsend. Understanding and setting healthy limits.

Websites And Organizations

Information:

- International Society for Traumatic Stress Studies: istss.org
- National Center for PTSD: ptsd.va.gov
- CPTSD Foundation: cptsdfoundation.org

Partner Support:

- Partners of Veterans with PTSD (national): partnersofvets.com
- NAMI (National Alliance on Mental Illness): nami.org
- Caregiver Action Network: caregiveraction.org

Support Groups

Online:

- Reddit: r/CPTSD_Partners
- Facebook groups (search "partners of trauma survivors" or "CPTSD family")
- Out of the Storm (online forum for CPTSD): outofthestorm.website

In-Person:

- Contact local mental health centers
- Ask your partner's therapist for referrals
- NAMI Family-to-Family programs

Finding A Therapist

Directories:

- Psychology Today: psychologytoday.com (filter by specialty)
- EMDR International Association: emdria.org
- IFS Directory: ifs-institute.com

Questions to Ask:

- What is your experience with trauma and PTSD?
- Do you understand Complex PTSD as distinct from PTSD?
- What approach do you use?
- Do you work with partners/family members?

Crisis Resources

US:

- 988 Suicide and Crisis Lifeline: Call or text 988
- Crisis Text Line: Text HOME to 741741
- Veterans Crisis Line: 1-800-273-8255, Press 1

International:

- International Association for Suicide Prevention: https://www.iasp.info/resources/Crisis_Centres/

Appendix C: Worksheets And Tools

Partner Self-Assessment

Rate each item from 0 (not at all) to 4 (extremely):

Emotional Impact: ___ I feel emotionally exhausted from supporting my partner ___ I have nightmares or intrusive thoughts about their trauma ___ I feel numb or unable to experience positive emotions ___ My worldview has become more negative ___ I feel hopeless about the future

Physical Impact: ___ I have sleep problems ___ I have new or worsening physical symptoms ___ I've neglected my own health care ___ My eating or exercise patterns have changed negatively

Relational Impact: ___ I've withdrawn from friends and family ___ I feel isolated ___ My other relationships have suffered ___ I've lost interest in activities I used to enjoy

Score Interpretation: 0-15: Monitor, implement self-care 16-30: Significant stress, seek additional support 31+: High distress, professional help recommended

---

Trigger Mapping Template

Known Triggers:

Trigger	Warning Signs	What Helps	What Makes It Worse
Example: Criticism	Gets quiet, shoulders tense	Reassurance, space	Defending or explaining

Times of Day/Year That Are Hard:

_____

People Who Are Triggering:

_____

Environments That Are Difficult:

_____
_____

Boundary Planning Worksheet

Boundary I need to set:

_____

Why this boundary matters for my wellbeing:

_____

How I will communicate this boundary:

_____

What I will do if the boundary is crossed:

_____

Anticipated reaction from my partner:

_____

How I will respond to that reaction:

197

Support I need to maintain this boundary:

_____

_____

Self-Care Audit

Physical care (sleep, nutrition, exercise, medical): Current status: _____ One thing I could improve: _____

Emotional care (therapy, processing, support): Current status: _____ One thing I could improve: _____

Social care (friends, family, community): Current status: _____ One thing I could improve: _____

Personal identity (interests, hobbies, goals beyond caregiving): Current status: _____ One thing I could improve: _____

Spiritual/meaning (whatever gives you sense of purpose): Current status: _____ One thing I could improve: _____

Holiday Survival Planner

Holiday/Event: _____

Potential triggers for my partner:

_____

Events we will attend:

198

Time limits for each:

Exit strategy (transportation, excuse, signal):

Support people who will be there:

Self-care planned before:

Recovery time planned after:

Glossary

4F Responses: The four survival responses to trauma: Fight, Flight, Freeze, and Fawn. Developed by Pete Walker to describe how people with complex trauma respond to perceived threats.

Attachment Style: The pattern of relating to intimate others that develops based on early experiences with caregivers. Styles include secure, anxious, avoidant, and disorganized.

C-PTSD (Complex PTSD): A condition resulting from prolonged, repeated trauma, especially in childhood, characterized by symptoms of PTSD plus emotional dysregulation, negative self-concept, and relationship difficulties.

Dissociation: A disconnection between normally integrated mental processes. Can include feeling detached from one's body, emotions, or surroundings.

Earned Secure Attachment: Developing secure attachment patterns in adulthood despite insecure attachment in childhood, usually through therapy and healthy relationships.

Emotional Flashback: A sudden regression into the overwhelming emotional states of childhood trauma, without visual memories. The person experiences intense fear, shame, or despair that belongs to the past but feels present.

Fawn Response: A survival response involving people-pleasing, self-abandonment, and prioritizing others' needs to maintain safety.

Inner Critic: The internalized voice of abusive or critical caregivers that attacks the person from within, generating shame and self-blame.

Secondary Traumatic Stress (STS): Trauma-like symptoms that develop from exposure to another person's traumatic experiences. Common in caregivers and loved ones of trauma survivors.

Toxic Shame: A pervasive sense of being fundamentally defective or worthless, as opposed to healthy shame about specific behaviors.

Trigger: Any stimulus that activates trauma responses. Can be a person, place, sound, smell, sensation, or situation that resembles aspects of the original trauma.

Window of Tolerance: The zone of arousal in which a person can function effectively. Trauma survivors often have a narrow window and can easily become hyper-aroused (activated) or hypo-aroused (shut down).

References

American Psychiatric Association. (2013). Diagnostic and statistical manual of mental disorders (5th ed.). American Psychiatric Publishing.

Bowlby, J. (1969). Attachment and loss: Vol. 1. Attachment. Basic Books.

Bowlby, J. (1988). A secure base: Parent-child attachment and healthy human development. Basic Books.

Bride, B. E., Robinson, M. M., Yegidis, B., & Figley, C. R. (2004). Development and validation of the Secondary Traumatic Stress Scale. Research on Social Work Practice, 14(1), 27-35. https://doi.org/10.1177/1049731503254106

Brown, B. (2012). Daring greatly: How the courage to be vulnerable transforms the way we live, love, parent, and lead. Gotham Books.

Cloitre, M., Garvert, D. W., Brewin, C. R., Bryant, R. A., & Maercker, A. (2013). Evidence for proposed ICD-11 PTSD and complex PTSD: A latent profile analysis. European Journal of Psychotraumatology, 4(1), 20706. https://doi.org/10.3402/ejpt.v4i0.20706

Cloitre, M., Stovall-McClough, K. C., Nooner, K., Zorbas, P., Cherry, S., Jackson, C. L., ... & Petkova, E. (2010). Treatment for PTSD related to childhood abuse: A randomized controlled trial. American Journal of Psychiatry, 167(8), 915-924. https://doi.org/10.1176/appi.ajp.2010.09081247

Cloud, H., & Townsend, J. (1992). Boundaries: When to say yes, how to say no to take control of your life. Zondervan.

Cohen, S., & Wills, T. A. (1985). Stress, social support, and the buffering hypothesis. Psychological Bulletin, 98(2), 310-357. https://doi.org/10.1037/0033-2909.98.2.310

Figley, C. R. (1995). Compassion fatigue: Coping with secondary traumatic stress disorder in those who treat the traumatized. Brunner/Mazel.

Ford, J. D., & Courtois, C. A. (2014). Complex PTSD, affect dysregulation, and borderline personality disorder. Borderline Personality Disorder and Emotion Dysregulation, 1, 9. https://doi.org/10.1186/2051-6673-1-9

Friedman, M. J. (2013). Finalizing PTSD in DSM-5: Getting here from there and where to go next. Journal of Traumatic Stress, 26(5), 548-556. https://doi.org/10.1002/jts.21840

Gottman, J. M. (1999). The seven principles for making marriage work. Crown Publishers.

Hazan, C., & Shaver, P. (1987). Romantic love conceptualized as an attachment process. Journal of Personality and Social Psychology, 52(3), 511-524. https://doi.org/10.1037/0022-3514.52.3.511

Herman, J. L. (1992). Trauma and recovery: The aftermath of violence, from domestic abuse to political terror. Basic Books.

Johnson, S. M. (2002). Emotionally focused couple therapy with trauma survivors: Strengthening attachment bonds. Guilford Press.

Johnson, S. M. (2008). Hold me tight: Seven conversations for a lifetime of love. Little, Brown Spark.

LeDoux, J. E. (2015). Anxious: Using the brain to understand and treat fear and anxiety. Viking.

Main, M., & Hesse, E. (1990). Parents' unresolved traumatic experiences are related to infant disorganized attachment status. In

M. T. Greenberg, D. Cicchetti, & E. M. Cummings (Eds.), Attachment in the preschool years (pp. 161-182). University of Chicago Press.

Maltz, W. (2012). The sexual healing journey: A guide for survivors of sexual abuse (3rd ed.). William Morrow.

Monson, C. M., & Fredman, S. J. (2012). Cognitive-behavioral conjoint therapy for PTSD: Harnessing the healing power of relationships. Guilford Press.

Monson, C. M., Fredman, S. J., Macdonald, A., Pukay-Martin, N. D., Resick, P. A., & Schnurr, P. P. (2012). Effect of cognitive-behavioral couple therapy for PTSD: A randomized controlled trial. JAMA, 308(7), 700-709. https://doi.org/10.1001/jama.2012.9307

Neff, K. D. (2011). Self-compassion: The proven power of being kind to yourself. William Morrow.

Porges, S. W. (2011). The polyvagal theory: Neurophysiological foundations of emotions, attachment, communication, and self-regulation. W. W. Norton & Company.

Roisman, G. I., Padrón, E., Sroufe, L. A., & Egeland, B. (2002). Earned-secure attachment status in retrospect and prospect. Child Development, 73(4), 1204-1219. https://doi.org/10.1111/1467-8624.00467

Schwartz, R. C. (2021). No bad parts: Healing trauma and restoring wholeness with the Internal Family Systems model. Sounds True.

Shapiro, F. (2018). Eye movement desensitization and reprocessing (EMDR) therapy: Basic principles, protocols, and procedures (3rd ed.). Guilford Press.

Siegel, D. J. (2012). The developing mind: How relationships and the brain interact to shape who we are (2nd ed.). Guilford Press.

Teicher, M. H., & Samson, J. A. (2016). Annual research review: Enduring neurobiological effects of childhood abuse and neglect. Journal of Child Psychology and Psychiatry, 57(3), 241-266. https://doi.org/10.1111/jcpp.12507

van der Kolk, B. A. (2014). The body keeps the score: Brain, mind, and body in the healing of trauma. Viking.

Walker, P. (2013). Complex PTSD: From surviving to thriving. Azure Coyote Publishing.

Watkins, L. E., Sprang, K. R., & Rothbaum, B. O. (2018). Treating PTSD: A review of evidence-based psychotherapy interventions. Frontiers in Behavioral Neuroscience, 12, 258. https://doi.org/10.3389/fnbeh.2018.00258

Webb, J. (2012). Running on empty: Overcome your childhood emotional neglect. Morgan James Publishing.

Werner, E. E. (1995). Resilience in development. Current Directions in Psychological Science, 4(3), 81-85. https://doi.org/10.1111/1467-8721.ep10772327

World Health Organization. (2019). International statistical classification of diseases and related health problems (11th ed.). https://icd.who.int/

Steiner, M. H., & Samson, J. A. (2019). Annual research review: Enduring neurobiological effects of childhood abuse and neglect. Journal of Child Psychology and Psychiatry, 57(3), 241–266. https://doi.org/10.1111/jcpp.12507